Heartwarming CHRISTMAS STORIES

Heartwarming CHRISTMAS STORIES

A COZY COLLECTION
OF FICTION
FOR THE HOLIDAYS

RiverOak®
Good News in Fiction

COOK COMMUNICATIONS MINISTRIES
Colorado Springs, Colorado • Paris, Ontario
KINGSWAY COMMUNICATIONS LTD
Eastbourne, England

RiverOak® is an imprint of
Cook Communications Ministries, Colorado Springs, CO 80918
Cook Communications, Paris, Ontario
Kingsway Communications, Eastbourne, England

HEARTWARMING CHRISTMAS STORIES
© 2006 Cook Communications Ministries

For individual story credits and copyrights, please see page 187.

All stories in this book are works of fiction. Names, characters, places, and incidents are either products of the authors' imaginations or used fictitiously. Any similarity to actual people, organizations, and/or events is purely coincidental.

Cover Design: Koechel Peterson & Associates, Inc.

First Printing, 2006
Printed in the United States of America

2 3 4 5 6 7 8 9 10 Printing/Year 10 09 08 07 06

All Scripture quotations, unless otherwise noted, are taken from the *Holy Bible, New International Version®. NIV®.* Copyright © 1973, 1978, 1984 by International Bible Society. Used by permission of Zondervan. All rights reserved. Scripture quotations marked KJV are taken from the King James Version of the Bible. (Public Domain.)

ISBN-13: 978-1-58919-095-5
ISBN-10: 1-58919-095-5

LCCN: 2006904672

For Ammar

Contents

ACKNOWLEDGMENTS

Special thanks to our vendor partners who provided the quality manufacturing of this book:

Advanta Graphics—New York, NY

Bang Printing—Brainerd, MN

THE MIRACLE YOU HOLD IN YOUR HANDS

Today is a good day for nine-year-old Ammar. For four months his home has been a hospital bed in Baghdad, Iraq. For four months terminal leukemia has ravaged his little body, damaging his facial nerves so badly that the muscles in his mouth can no longer smile.

But his eyes can.

They are sparkling as Ammar's hands lovingly caress the beautiful, thick book of cartoons that has just been placed on his bed. The cartoons tell more than stories of superheroes or silly animals—they tell the story of God and life in vivid scenes and child-appropriate words. And Ammar is just one of thousands of children in Iraq to receive a free, brand-new copy of *The Picture Bible* in his own language. In the comic-book style pages of *The Picture Bible*, Ammar—and his family—will discover the colors of creation, the heroes of faith, and most importantly, the great good news of Jesus Christ's life, death, and resurrection.

All this in a tiny bed at the Children's Teaching Hospital in Baghdad, Iraq.

Today is a good day for the members of the Evangelical League of Cuba, a thriving Christian church located in Havana. This group started out as a simple house church where a few believers gathered to worship Jesus. Now it is a three-thousand-member community of Christians who meet each week in a home that's been fully remodeled into a church building. On Sundays the place is so packed with people that many teenagers actually stand outside the church and listen through the windows in order to participate in worship.

There are visitors from the United States at the Evangelical League service today. They are representatives from Cook Communications Ministries International (CCMI), and they have a special interest in the goings-on at this place. Jose Lopez, president of the Bible Commission of Cuba, holds up a familiar book. In the past months, weeks, and years, CCMI has donated thousands of copies of

The New Testament Picture Bible to churches all over the Cuban landscape.

"These people," Jose says, gesturing toward the American visitors, "are the ones who have provided these books for the Evangelical League of Cuba."

The response is immediate—and deafening. Three thousand people break into grateful applause, cheering, and clapping. The ovation is so loud and boisterous that it soon evolves into an extended, rhythmic chanting that disrupts the entire meeting until the people finally calm down.

And everyone is smiling.

Today is another good day—and this time it's because of you.

You see, the book you now hold in your hands is part of the miracle that Ammar experienced, part of the joy from the congregation at the Evangelical League of Cuba, and part of the ongoing work that Cook Communications Ministries International is doing around the world. For instance, in 2004 alone CCMI printed and distributed over 5 million pieces of free Christian literature to equip and strengthen the church in places like China, Cuba, Vietnam, India, Sudan, and Iraq. Each year, CCMI also hosts hundreds of foreign publishing professionals from scores of different countries for intensive ten-day training seminars on how to spread the message of Christ in their respective homelands.

Oh, and those powerful *Picture Bibles*? Over the years, CCMI has printed and given away over 81 million copies in more than 140 languages, making the story of Jesus accessible to children—literally—all over the world.

That's why this book, *Heartwarming Christmas Stories*, is such a special thing. You see, the publisher, authors, and illustrators have decided to make this more than just a book of heartwarming, hope-filled stories for the holidays (although it certainly fits that bill!). In a unique fit of generosity, everyone involved with *Heartwarming Christmas Stories* has agreed to donate all profits from this book to the ongoing ministry of CCMI around the world. And 100 percent of every dollar earned from this book will be translated into life-changing projects like the distribution of *Picture Bibles* in Iraq, the donation of Sunday school materials to churches in Cuba, and many, many more.

So you see, today is a very good day. Today you have gained a wonderful collection of Christmas stories written by some of the world's best Christian authors—their special gift to you. As a result, thousands of children and churches across the world will hear anew the much-needed message that Jesus loves them, Jesus died for them, and Jesus rose from the dead to give them life evermore— your special gift to them.

So merry Christmas, dear reader, and thank you for your willingness to join us in wishing the world a merry Christmas during this joyous time of the year.

After all, people like you put a smile into Ammar's beautiful eyes.

Blessings!

—Mike Nappa, editor

SIGMUND BROUWER

CHRISTMAS EXPRESS

WHEN I BROKE OVER the hill and saw the wagon down below at the river, I told myself to stay at full gallop. With a snowstorm close behind, night approaching, and five miles to go, I had more things to worry about than a dumb farmer traveling on a day like this.

He heard the thundering of my horse's hooves and looked up. He began to wave his hat as I approached. I didn't lift my hands from the reins to wave back. Riding at full gallop takes plenty of concentration.

"Hey, mister!" he shouted as soon as he began to understand I meant to keep riding. "Hey, mister! I need help!"

Not from me, I told myself. Pony Express riders had strict instructions. Deliver the mail at any cost.

He kept waving and shouting. I shut my ears against his voice. But I made the mistake of looking over as my horse slowed to enter the river just downstream from his wagon. I saw the man's face, the slump of his shoulders like he'd just lost all hope because I was passing him by.

I pulled back on the reins.

Just one minute, I told myself. I'd stop long enough to explain why I couldn't help. He'd understand. Everyone had heard of the Pony Express and how we were able to deliver a letter from California to Missouri in an unbelievable eight days.

"Thanks, mister," he said as my horse stamped its hooves and pranced. "I'm in a terrible fix here. My horse has gone lame. Short of pulling this wagon myself, I cain't get home."

This man wore a chewed-up floppy hat. His dark beard covered most of his face. His clothes were worn and ragged. I found it interesting he called me mister. I'm barely sixteen, and except for a wild cuss named Bill Cody, I am the youngest rider in all of the Pony Express.

"Sorry, not much I can do," I told him. I pointed at the mailbags on my saddle. "I ride for the Express. They're expecting me ahead."

He nodded. If he lived somewhere nearby he'd know of the Pony Express station at the Weyburn ranch where fresh horses were kept ready for riders coming and going both directions. A rider covered three stations, each ten to fifteen miles apart, changing horses at each station.

This was my last leg. I'd come down the foothills of the

Rockies, heading east across the plains. Ahead at the station a fine young woman awaited me. Lucy Weyburn. She was as sweet on me as I was on her. Seeing her tonight would be extra special, as I had a red silk scarf wrapped in fancy paper as a Christmas gift for her.

"Mister," he said, "you can see the snow is almost on us."

I could, of course. The approaching clouds were so dark that the mountains behind were almost lost to sight. I'd been racing the weather since leaving the last station, figuring if I kept good pace I'd be fine.

"I hope you understand," he said, "it ain't me I'm worried for. It's my wife and my four children. I went into town yesterday and promised 'em I'd be home by tonight. If I don't show … when the snow hits they'll be scared I'm lost or got took by Indians."

"I don't see what I can do," I said. "We abide by strict regulations. Just bringing my horse to a stop like this could lose me my job."

"Mister," he said, pulling his hat from his head and holding it at his chest, "if you could just go a half mile out of your way, you'd be doing me as much favor as a man could ask."

I shook my head no. Pony Express had rules.

"Someone should be along," I said. "This trail gets used often enough."

"On the eve of Christmas?" he asked. "I ain't seen anyone for hours, and I was surprised to see you. I'd have started walking, 'cept with the Indian trouble I cain't leave behind my wagon and all the supplies. Cash money's real scarce right now. Without these supplies, we won't last the winter."

I nibbled my lower lip. It's a habit I've got when I don't rightly know what to do.

"Some five miles ahead and directly along your way," he told me, "you'll see a rock tower guarded by a tall pine. Turn north along a dry creek bed, and you'll see the homestead in a half mile. Hardly out of your way. With the horse you've got, it would take no time at all to let my family know where I'm at."

I kept nibbling. The first flakes of snow began drifting down into our faces.

He continued, twisting his hat in his hands. "As soon's the storm passes, my wife, she'll send the oldest to the neighbor. And he'll come back with a horse to help me out. I'll be fine here waiting. I got blankets and a rifle. It's them I'm worried about. If they think I'm hurt or took by Indians, my boys might come looking for me and perish themselves. They's just young."

I didn't want to tell him yes. There were the regulations. And darkness and a storm to beat. And Lucy was waiting for me.

"Mister," he said, looking up at me high on my horse. "I'm sorry to beg. I do know Pony Express riders cain't stop for nothing. But I don't know what else I can do 'cept throw myself on your mercy."

I finally nodded. Some things were more important than a job. "Consider it done," I said.

"God bless you!" He hesitated. "Just in case it takes a while to ride out the storm, can you deliver some presents? I promised them something for Christmas, and a man hates breaking promises to his children."

I nodded again. The snow was sweeping in harder, and I wanted to be on my way.

The man ran to his wagon. He dug into a box and came back with four small packages, wrapped in plain brown paper, tied with cheap string.

"One for each of my boys," he said.

I took them and slipped them inside my jacket.

"Thank you kindly," he said. "Comes the day I can do the same for you or anyone else, I'll return the favor."

I waited. I was expecting him to come up with another gift, one for his wife.

He half frowned. "Something wrong?"

"I'll be happy to take along the present for your woman," I told him.

"We're going through tough times," he said, staring off. "Something little would put a sparkle back in her eyes, but all I could afford was a few trinkets for the boys. I'm hoping she'll understand."

I felt his shame. Like a coward, I saluted good-bye, wheeled my horse around, and splashed it through the river and away from his misery.

It didn't take long to reach the rock tower. If Pony Express horses are one thing, they are fast and tough.

I was fine too, even with the snow falling heavy in the purple light of dusk. I'd ridden through plenty worse. It was my job, no different from every other Pony Express man in the country. We weren't to let snow or hail or heat or Indian attacks stop us. It was as simple as that.

The snow began to fall so heavy that the rock tower was already coated white when I got there. I found the dry creek bed easy enough and was grateful for it. The way it was snowing, I'd need something to follow to get me back to the rock tower.

I rode hard with snow whipping across my horse. My arms and gloves became as white as the ground. I knew that once there I wasn't going to waste any time delivering my news. If I didn't get back to the main trail quick, I'd risk getting lost.

A half mile at a gallop don't take long. There was a light in the single window of a cabin and as I got close, I could see it was a candle.

I jumped right down from my horse. I didn't even bother to brush the snow off my coat and hat and arms. I heard singing inside. I knocked on the door.

A small woman with a tired face and a shy smile opened it. Behind her, I saw the heads of four boys. She shooed them, and they returned to peek around her. I guessed the oldest to be eight years old.

"Hello," she said. I saw her eyes move up and down as she looked at the snow that covered me. She stepped back from the doorway. "Come in. You must be freezing. We've got some soup, and you're welcome to it."

"Thank you kindly, but no," I said. "My name's Jesse, and I ride for the Pony Express. Your husband—"

She brought her hands to her face. "He's not hurt! We've been waiting on him, singing Christmas carols to pass time and—"

"He's fine, ma'am." I explained all of it to her.

"That sets me at ease," she said. Still, her face looked tired and sad.

I took off a snowy glove and pulled a brown package from inside my jacket.

"He asked me to deliver this," I said. She smiled like I'd handed her a bar of gold.

"Merry Christmas," I said, giving her the other three packages. "For the boys."

"Merry Christmas," she said back to me. Her eyes kept going to my coat. But I didn't have anything for her.

"Well," I said, "I've got to be moving on. Can't let the storm get the best of me."

"I understand," she said. The smile had left her face. It near broke my heart, thinking of how she must be struggling to raise four boys out here. I remembered how the man had said he wanted to put a sparkle back in her face.

"'Course," I said, "there is one last present."

I reached into my jacket a final time. I pulled out Lucy's fancy wrapped silk scarf and set in it her hands. She'd thank her husband tomorrow, and I hoped he'd be smart enough not to let on what happened.

Whatever that scarf cost me, it was worth triple to see the joy in her face.

"Ma'am," I said, tipping my snowy hat good-bye.

As she slowly closed the door, I heard the littlest boy speak. "Momma," he asked. "Was the man in white an angel?"

"Yes, Johnny," I heard her say, "I believe he was."

Hard as it snowed, I was warm the rest of my ride into the night.

WANDA LUTTRELL

A CARDINAL, BLOODRED

HE WAS BACK, PECKING on the glass of the kitchen door, his hypnotic black eyes peering in at her, willing her to comply with his demands.

"What do you want?" she asked aloud. The cardinal stared at her through the center of the Christmas wreath hanging inside the door. *He looks like a bright red Christmas ornament himself,* Carrie thought, but his glittery eyes were hard and threatening.

Nonsense! she thought. *How threatening can one tiny bird be?* Laughing, she tried to stare him down but had to turn away in defeat. Behind her, she could hear him attacking the glass with renewed intensity. She turned and saw him beating his wings against the pane, and a tingle of fear gathered at the base of her neck.

"What do you want?" she whispered, starting for the kitchen door. The baby cried out, and she stopped uncertainly. "Go away!" she ordered the bird, waving one hand at him as she turned to the hallway that led to Marty's room. The baby must have cried out in his sleep, she decided, for a glance into his room showed him still sleeping on his stomach in his crib.

She could still hear the cardinal back there, beating at the glass as she went on down the hall to the master bedroom. "What's the matter with that crazy bird?" she asked Martin, handing him clean underwear to pack for another interminable cross-country trip. "At first, I thought he was cracking sun-flower seeds on the window's hard surface, but he has nothing in his beak."

"He's vain as a peacock!" Martin laughed. "When I went out to start the truck, he was perched on the side mirror sup-port admiring himself in the glass. He probably sees his reflection in the window."

"But why does he attack it so?"

Martin stuffed clean socks into his leather carryall and zipped it shut. "Maybe he thinks he sees a rival in the glass. Maybe he's the cocky little bantam rooster of the cardinal family, ready to take on the whole world."

She could see that Martin was identifying with the bird now—the world challenger who had chucked his teaching position and climbed into the cab of an eighteen-wheeler to enable his daughters to attend the best Christian college in the state and to enable his wife to stay home with their Johnny-come-lately son. And partly, she suspected, to thumb his nose at a society that paid its truck drivers more than it paid the teachers of its future citizens.

"Well, he gives me the creeps," she insisted, "with that evil pecking."

"What's so evil about fighting back?" Martin answered belligerently, identifying fully with the bird now.

She smiled up at him. "Nothing, sweetheart, so long as you know what you are fighting. And you always do," she added honestly. "You always know which money changers should be thrown out of the temple."

He ignored that. "Apples to the west coast and oranges back," he sighed, juggling the carryall and an extra pair of boots as he blew Marty a kiss from the bedroom doorway. He turned to her, his eyes troubled. "Will you be all right?"

"Of course, we will!" she laughed, following him down the hall to the front door. "I've got the four-wheel drive if I have to go … anywhere." She veered away from voicing the concern that the baby's cold might develop into the pneumonia they had dreaded since those first scary moments after his birth when his lung had collapsed. "He's just got a little cold, hon," she reassured him.

"The county road crew has scraped and salted the roads, but from the looks of that sky, we could get another ice storm. Don't forget, the truck tires are slick," he reminded her. "I've been meaning to put new snow tires on, but with the girls' tuition …"

"Whoa! Where's all that faith you're always preaching to me?" she interrupted, reaching up to give him a hug. "We'll be fine."

He drew her to him, gave her a lingering kiss, then opened the door and went out.

"Have a good trip," she said, watching him cautiously maneuver the icy stoop and then the sidewalk. "And hurry back!" she called. "You've got to be here to put up the tree before the girls get home on the twenty-third!"

He gave a backward wave to acknowledge that responsibility and climbed into the cab. She watched until he pulled out of the driveway on to the county road, then she shut the door.

Alone in the house with the sleeping baby, she again became aware of the cardinal's furious pecking. He appeared first at one window, then another, stopping to peer in at her with beady, malevolent eyes.

Maybe he's trying to tell me the feeder's empty, she thought hopefully. Obligingly, she pulled on boots, coat, and gloves, picked up the bucket of sunflower seeds by the back door, and carried it outside.

"You crazy bird!" she called to the cardinal, his bright red topknot just visible now from the tangled naked branches of the forsythia bush. "This feeder is over half full!"

The cardinal ignored that. "I'm talking to you, you rascal!" she laughed, filling the feeder anyway. Back inside, she closed the kitchen door behind her, enjoying the spicy tangerine scent of Douglas fir that the movement released from the wreath. She set the bucket beside the door, noting that it held only a couple more fillings. She hoped Martin would be home before the seed was gone. The ice had covered all the available natural food sources.

Suddenly, she heard the delicate rattle of sleet against the windowpanes. "If he isn't, you'll just have to fend for yourself!" she told the cardinal, back now at the kitchen window. "I'm not taking my baby out in this weather on these roads to buy bird seed, no matter how much I like birds. Present company excepted," she added.

The cardinal stared in at her arrogantly. She had to admit he was a handsome bird. *But Lucifer was the most beautiful of all the angels,* she thought, and shivered.

She could hear him out there all through the afternoon as she hung silver bells from the interior archways and arranged the fragile figures of the Nativity scene in its traditional niche in the brick fireplace wall that covered one whole end of the keeping room.

The vegetable soup bubbling on the stove had steamed up all of the windows, but she couldn't hear the cardinal. She cleared a spot in the steam, expecting to meet his black, unblinking gaze, but the window ledge was empty.

The enormity of her relief was absurd. What danger could there be from one small bird? However, she knew her fears were not for herself but for Marty. "That's irrational!" she told herself sternly. Unless the bird got inside and pecked him in the face, he certainly was no threat to her baby.

She turned her thoughts deliberately back to preparations for Christmas. The days were slipping by. She supposed she should get the boxes of ornaments down from the attic and have them ready for the girls to put on the tree when Martin had it ready. She smiled, thinking of how the girls always enjoyed decorating the tree, exclaiming over each treasured ornament they had collected through the years.

They'd want a fire in the fireplace, and nonalcoholic eggnog sprinkled with nutmeg to toast the tree in all its glory when they were done. Did she have any nutmeg left after yesterday's baking she wondered, going to the spice rack at the end of the cooking bar to check the bottle.

Assured that her store of nutmeg was adequate, she went down the hall to check on the baby. He was sleeping on his back now with all the covers off. She covered him and bent to drop a kiss on his forehead beneath the bright corn-silk hair.

Gasping, she drew back, her lips almost burned by the contact with his skin. Panic rose inside her. She withdrew the covers, praying as she reached for the thermometer. She jumped at the sudden pecking at the bedroom window and watched in dismay as the thermometer fell and shattered on the hardwood floor.

She grabbed the Tylenol, forced Marty's lips open, squeezed a double dose of the red liquid into his mouth, and held it shut until he swallowed. He whimpered and thrashed from side to side. Her prayer was incoherent as she ran to the bathroom for the rubbing alcohol. She rubbed his hot little body with alcohol, then soaked a washcloth in cold water and placed it across his forehead.

Too soon the cloth was hot, and she ran back to the bathroom for more cold water, forcing herself to pray slowly, one thought following another in rational order, willing a belief she could not feel.

Suddenly, the words from Hosea 9:16 were in her mind: "I will slay your cherished offspring"!

God was talking to the Ephraimites in that verse she reminded herself quickly. One can prove anything by taking a verse out of context. *God surely would not punish me by slaying an innocent child!*

In memory, she could hear her grandmother's soft Southern voice. "A bird in the house is a sign of death," she had said when that swallow fell down the chimney and nearly beat itself to death against the windowpane before Grandma could catch it in her apron and put it outside. She couldn't remember if the prediction had come true.

Grandma and her "signs," Carrie thought nervously. Old wives' tales. Sometimes, though, they had proved true. "An unwound clock strikin' means somebody will be dead before another midnight passes," Grandma had said, and Grandpa Richards had died the morning after that long-unwound clock in the attic had struck.

"This is just a little red bird, for Pete's sake!" she said aloud. "He doesn't really mean any harm." But his baleful eye, watching her as she bathed the baby in alcohol again, denied that. "Anyway, he's not in the house, and he can't get in!" she told herself firmly.

The bird's determined pecking mocked her words. Suddenly aware of the thinness of the glass, of their exposure in the softly lit room, she jerked the curtains across the window. Still, she could hear him out there, pecking away.

She snatched the telephone receiver from its cradle and was greeted by dead silence. The line was out. Her first thought was that Martin would not be able to reach them with his nightly call. Then the reality of her situation hit. This country place they had chosen for the good of the children was two miles from the nearest neighbor. The telephone might be out for days. She couldn't even reach the doctor!

She turned to the baby and laid her hand on his still burning forehead. The medicine and the evaporating alcohol should have begun to lower the fever by now. Was it the cardinal's curse at work? Was it Hosea 9:16?

"Stop it!" she ordered. "If Martin were here ..." But he was miles away by now, pushing his rig to the limit to complete his run and get back to her and little Marty.

It was uncanny the way this baby neither of them had wanted had taken over their hearts. If anything happens to him now ...

"I will slay your cherished offspring."

"No, God, please!" she begged. "I didn't mean it! Not that way!"

When she had prayed that her unexpected pregnancy would end she hadn't thought of it as wanting a little person to die. The baby had been merely a faceless embryo, an unwanted intrusion into their lives just when both the girls were in college and she was preparing to return to the career she had abandoned in favor of full-time motherhood twenty years ago.

She remembered how trapped she had felt, how ashamed as she faced the shocked disbelief of her daughters, the smug complacency of relatives and friends. "By the time this child is fifteen, you and Martin will be nearing retirement age," more than one of them had pointed out. "Are you sure you will be able to cope with a teenager then?"

She hadn't even been sure she could cope with the terrible twos, much less the troubled teens. What if they encountered a repeat of Leslie's unhappy struggles with peer relationships or the bitter rebellion they had unexplainably experienced with Suzanne? Or perhaps this child would come up with some terrible ordeal of his own to put them through. She was just too tired—too old!

None of that had mattered, of course, once little Marty arrived. They all adored him, and Martin said they simply would trust God to get them through whatever lay ahead. But Martin didn't know the terrible guilty secret that lay between her and God, the death wish she had visited on her unborn child.

He didn't know how she had prayed for deliverance from the suspected pregnancy, how she had played a frantic "Bible roulette," letting the Bible fall open and searching the verses for some reassurance that she would not have to go through with this embarrassment that surely only happened to other women.

Then her eyes had fallen on Hosea 9:16: "Ephraim is blighted, their root is withered, they yield no fruit. Even if they bear children, I will slay their cherished offspring." Quickly she had moved to other verses, "a goose walking over her grave," as Grandma would have called that shiver down her spine. She didn't want the baby to die after they had grown to "cherish" him! Still, the curse had become hers: After they had grown to cherish him, this child would die.

"Do you think a murderer can be forgiven?" she had asked Martin one night as they watched a news story about the last-minute confession of a serial killer. Could she be forgiven for the murder in her heart and then the curse of Hosea 9:16 would be lifted?

"The Bible says that Jesus prayed for those who crucified him. I guess he can forgive anything if a person is truly sorry, Carrie," he had answered.

There's no doubt that I am truly sorry! she had thought.

"He can repent, accept Christ's salvation, and go to heaven," Martin had expounded, "but he still has to face the consequences of his crimes here." Her hopes had plummeted.

Carrie became aware that the baby's heavy breathing was the only sound in the room. She lifted the curtain. The sleet had stopped, and so had the pecking. The window ledge was empty. She looked out over the ice-encased world outside, shimmering like an earth-bound aurora borealis in the slanting rays of the setting sun. There, from a drooping middle branch of the ice-burdened white pine, the glittering jet black eyes in their ruby red setting watched the house.

Not ruby red, she thought in horror, *bloodred!* He was out there, waiting. But why? Then she wondered if the cardinal was merely a harbinger, to warn her that death stalked the house?

Suddenly, she knew she had to get the baby away from this house. She threw supplies into a diaper bag, grabbed Marty's snowsuit and stuffed him into it. He whimpered, his breathing ragged with fever.

She pulled on her parka, boots, and gloves and grabbed her purse and keys. She picked up the baby, feeling the threat gathering behind her as she ran down the stairs to the basement.

Carrie strapped Marty into his car seat and started the pickup. She opened the garage door, backed out onto the icy driveway, and put the gear in park. Holding onto the truck, she pulled down the garage door and locked it.

Back in the truck, she put it into reverse and gunned the motor, feeling the rear end fishtail sickeningly between the retaining walls. She jerked her foot off the accelerator. *Maybe I should have taken the car,* she thought, but not even front-wheel drive would help on this solid sheet of ice.

Cautiously, she pressed the accelerator, felt the wheels spin, then take hold. She backed slowly onto the turn-around and eased down the driveway. The rear end slid sideways as she pulled onto the county road. She jerked the wheel in the direction of the skid. The truck straightened, and she inched along the narrow road.

Surely the road crews had cleared the highway by now. If she could just make it down that one long, treacherous hill to the state road … She stopped the truck at the top of the hill and took a deep breath, her thoughts turning longingly to their snug little house. Did the evil eye of the cardinal still watch it, unaware that they had escaped? Did death itself still watch, or had he followed them?

The baby whimpered and tried to turn over. "Hold on, sweetheart," she soothed, easing the truck over the hill and into the first curve.

"I will slay your cherished offspring!"

Carrie gasped and jerked the wheel. The rear end of the truck lurched sideways, picking up speed as she frantically, uselessly, turned the wheel into the skid. She clutched the baby seat, repeating a broken litany of prayer as they whirled around, bounced off the cliff on one side, spun halfway around again, crossed the road, and slid into the ditch facing the way they had come. One headlight pointed skyward and the other focused cross-eyed into the cliff.

She turned to the baby, knowing in her heart that it had been futile to try to run from the wrath of God. With numb fingers, she unstrapped Marty's limp body and lifted it from the seat. She cradled him to her, grieving. She touched her lips to his forehead. Then she began to cry with gratitude and joy. The baby's forehead was damp. His fever had broken, and she could hear him snoring softly, peacefully asleep.

A familiar pattern of lights across the top of an eighteen-wheeler crawled toward them up the hill. A door slammed, and she felt the door of the pickup open. Two strong arms encircled her and the baby.

"When I saw those lights go crazy, I knew somebody was in for it," Martin said, "but when I saw the truck and knew …" His voice broke. "Praise the Lord!" he breathed.

"Praise the Lord!" she echoed, her thoughts not so much on their escape from the wreck as on a God who could forgive— thorns, jeers, nails, and, surely, the ugly guilt that had caused her foolish fears.

"I'm giving it up, Carrie," Martin was saying as he lifted her and the baby into the cab of the other truck. "When I couldn't reach you, with little Marty sick …" He held them to him, babbling about selling the rig and putting the money into the bank for the girl's tuition, getting a teaching job.

She became aware that Martin had stopped talking. He was looking at her as though he expected an answer. "Where were you going on a night like this, Carrie?" he repeated. "It must have been important."

The image of a bloodred cardinal with bright black eyes flashed across her mind. As Martin went around to the other side and climbed into the cab beside them, she tried to think of a way to put it all into words. "It was …"

Marty opened his eyes, happily murmured, "Da-da! Twuck!" and sank back into sleep. She smoothed the damp corn-silk hair back from his face.

"… just a little red bird fighting his image in the glass," she said, "and Hosea 9:16 was for the Ephraimites."

"Are you all right?" Martin asked worriedly. "Is Marty …?"

She shook her head, trying to smile through the tears. "Marty and I are fine," she assured him, laying her hand over his on the gearshift. "Just fine," she repeated, sure of it.

T. L. HIGLEY

BROKEN PIECES

I HATE THAT COLD stone beast.

I pressed my forehead against the chilly glass pane of my darkened museum workroom and watched a light blink on inside the New City Church across the street.

Okay, I didn't hate the church. Not truly. But I knew that it would soon open its doors to righteous Christmas Eve worshippers, while others of us, lost in the guilt of past mistakes, would long for redemption from distant places across the street.

I breathed a patch of fog onto the glass, then pushed away and turned back to my worktable where broken artifacts were still able to be repaired. I shared this cramped, street-level workroom in the museum with two other restorers, but they had long left for the holiday, escaping cluttered workspaces, fleeing to filled-up lives.

The partially restored clay pot I'd been working on today still lay in seven pieces, but my time was up. I circled the table and placed the pieces back into their foam-cushioned box. I would finish perfecting it after the holiday.

If I'm around that long.

I use four different types of adhesive in my work, and I took a moment to line the bottles up like plastic soldiers at attention, guarding the edge of my table. I placed soiled paper into the trash bin, swept clay dust into the palm of my hand, and then brushed it into the trash as well. I filed my notes from the day and sharpened three pencils before putting them into the drawer. I took a deep breath and studied my workspace, then nudged one of the adhesive bottles forward into formation. Across the semidarkness of the room, my cell phone rang. I pulled my tan purse from the counter and retrieved the blinking phone, studying the incoming number. Kristina.

I opened the phone. "Hello?"

"Natalee? Are you still at work?"

"I'm leaving now."

"Oh, honey, I'm so sorry to do this to you …"

I exhaled and waited. Across the street the first saint scurried up to the oak doors of the church.

"It's little Toby, Natalee. The poor guy woke up with a cough this morning."

"Is he okay?" Kristina's new baby had lit up my coworker's world and taken over her life.

"The doctor says he'll be fine, but he's not sleeping well, and he's so cranky. Michael just got off work, and he's trying to rest …"

"It's fine, Kristina. I don't need to come."

Kristina paused. "I feel so bad, honey. I hate to think of your spending Christmas Eve alone."

Not the first time. I leaned against the counter, legs a little weak. "Don't worry about it. I'll be fine."

"We'll have you over really soon when Toby is feeling better."

"That'll be great, Kristina. Have a good Christmas."

"You, too, girlfriend."

I snapped my phone shut and pressed the cool metal against my forehead. I didn't fault Kristina. Husband and baby were more than enough Christmas Eve for anyone. No need for a messed-up coworker with no place better to go.

Stop it, Natalee. You're a pathetic, whining idiot.

Well, perhaps I was. But it was the truth. I returned the phone to my purse, and my fingers brushed the sharp edge of the days-old office party invitation. I pulled it out and studied the cheery Santa sticker in the bottom corner and the green-inked "Natalie" scrawled in the middle. I flicked a finger against those last two letters. In my world of medium build, medium brown hair, and medium talent, the spelling of my name is the only standout feature about me. But my boss, Hank, hadn't noticed and used the common spelling. I hadn't attended the party last night. No one mentioned my absence today.

Would they miss me if I never came back to work?

I leaned a hip against the counter once more and closed my eyes.

There's a reason for the increase in suicides at Christmas.

There's only one place in my world where things seem to be put right. It's in the ancient pieces I restore, displayed in the floors above my workroom for visitors to admire. Tonight, a sudden desire to see one of my whole pieces filled me. To see something, anything, I had done right. Perhaps to stop the frightening wave of hopelessness that threatened to sweep me into despair.

I locked the workroom behind me and drifted down the dark hallway. I was probably the last person out of here tonight. Somewhere in the building a security guard no doubt wandered, shining his flashlight into dim corners and shadowed alcoves. I tread carefully to the stairs, heading for the third floor's Roman, Etruscan, and Greek halls. The stairwell door clanged behind me, intruding into the peace of the building. I winced.

Hope the security guard's unarmed.

The pieces in the rooms above me were priceless, worthy of theft. I lapsed into philosophy as I trudged upward, wondering what makes a person priceless. No one had tried to steal my heart in a long while. Or even win it fairly for crying out loud.

But if priceless were to be defined, it would look nothing like the irreparable, jagged edges of my life.

I reached the third level, a little breathless, and opened the door into the Mesopotamian hall. The room was dark, with only the exit signs and an occasional forgotten exhibit case light to illuminate the room. I glided around the free-standing glass exhibits to the other side of the hall, through another domed room, to the entrance of the Roman World exhibits.

Here I paused, considering alarming the security guard by turning on the lights in the room to better see the piece I was most proud of.

I breathed the stale air and thought, *perhaps this would be a fitting place to put an end to ... things.*

Plaster statues lined the walls of the Roman World, and counter-height glass exhibits squatted around the room. To one side was a scale model of a Roman villa, again under glass. In the center of the room stood a seven-foot wall, with fourth- and fifth-century manuscripts displayed on both sides. The wall blocked my view of the exhibits on the far side of the room. The piece I'd come to see was over there.

I moved to step into the room, but a sound on the other side of that wall stopped me. Just a whisper of a footfall against the floor. I waited. The shuffling sound came again and the room suddenly felt even darker. I wished for the security guard. Or did he stand on the other side of that wall himself?

A shadow moved away from the wall. I sucked in my breath and took a step backward. The figure moved slowly. I squinted through the darkness to identify it. The shadow moved toward a glass case. It seemed draped in a flowing fabric, ghostlike. What seemed like an arm passed over the case, hesitated, then drew back, holding something. The figure moved away then, toward the doors that led to the Etruscan hall. I waited until I was alone in the room then trotted to the glass display.

It was empty.

My heart rate jumped into overdrive. The attached plaque detailed the gladiator's sword and shield that should have lay there. I slid my fingers around the edges of the glass door. It pulled open in my hands easily. Unlocked. Too late I wondered if I should have left my fingerprints on the case.

I pushed it closed and glanced at the door where the intruder had disappeared. Had he already escaped the building?

Where was the security guard? Could I find him before the thief disappeared?

You're thinking of dying for nothing, girl; why not for something worthwhile?

I held my breath and willed heavy feet forward to the door.

It slid open in silence. I could see him again at the end of the Etruscan hall. The light was a little stronger here, and it was clear that it was a man dressed in some kind of floor-length robe. Odd outfit for an antiquities thief.

Should I confront him? To what end? Perhaps scare him into leaving his treasures behind and fleeing the museum? Not likely.

Well then, at least get a close enough look at him to help identify him later.

But in that moment he turned.

And I knew I was lost.

He wore a robe, yes, but it opened in front to reveal a short tunic, white and belted at the waist. On his head he wore the helmet of a Roman soldier, and in his hands he carried the sword and shield missing from its case. The light above a wall-mounted painting fell across his features. Black eyes glittered behind the mask of the helmet, and I shuddered to see the gaze fall upon me. The sword rose to chest-level, its lethal point directed at me. I inhaled deeply and summoned a courage I didn't own.

"What are you doing here?" I asked.

The man threw muscular shoulders back, and the robe fell away from his arms. "I am Antonio." He waved the sword in a small figure eight, as though warning me to come no farther.

"You shouldn't be here, Zorro," I said. The sarcasm flowed as habit, in spite of fear.

He lowered the sword only slightly. "I belong here as much as you do."

I tried a bluff. I looked back over my shoulder and called out, "Guard!"

Antonio waited, watching me. The silence of the Etruscan Hall continued, with no rescuer swooping in to tackle him.

I licked dry lips.

"You are afraid," Antonio said.

"You are stealing priceless artifacts."

Antonio looked at the sword in his hand, twisted it back and forth as though examining an old friend.

"Am I? This sword has served me well over many years."

"Served you well?" The guy was beginning to creep me out.

He tapped the shield he held. "As has this piece." His black eyes bore into mine, and his voice lowered to a whisper. "Come closer."

I swallowed but moved forward, drawn by his eyes.

When I stood only a few feet from him, he lifted a hand and traced a finger across a scar on his leather-covered chest. "This shield saved my life in the deadliest combat I faced." His eyes returned to mine. "Do you want to feel the leather? Feel how my opponent's blade nearly sliced through to my flesh?"

"That breastplate has been in this museum for years."

"And strapped to my body for more years than that."

"Who are you?"

"I am Antonio."

Right. "Are you saying that these things belonged to you—"

"In the eleventh year of Emperor Nero Claudius Drusus Germanicus."

A nervous laugh escaped my lips. "You're from the first century?" I wished I could see more than the eyes behind the helmet. As if in answer, Antonio pulled the helmet from his head.

I never expected the white hair and deeply lined features. Though his body was muscular, the face showed the passing of years, and I guessed his age to be at least sixty.

Antonio smiled. "You expected a younger warrior?"

I shook my head, unable to respond.

"I am not surprised. Gladiators do not often live to old age." He flourished the sword again, a smile forming. "But my weapons served me well, and I was able to buy my freedom."

He was insane, obviously. Senile. Or perhaps both. A white-haired man dressed as a Roman, brandishing weapons and claiming to be two thousand years old.

I should just leave, find the security guard, and let him deal with this loony guy. I turned away, watching behind me to keep track of that sword.

"Don't leave, Natalee."

I stopped. Turned back to him.

"How do you know my name?"

He motioned to a set of steps leading to the Greek display room. "Sit with me. You are alone, and it is not a night to be alone."

He moved to the steps then, sat down, and laid the sword and helmet on the step beside him. Those eyes, still so mesmerizing even in the lined face, turned on me and urged me to sit.

I lowered myself to the steps. *What am I doing?*

"Who are you?" I said again.

Antonio smiled and inclined his head toward the room of Greek pottery. "A person not unlike these pieces. Broken. Yet restored." He rubbed at a scar on his hand. "I suppose we are all broken in some way, aren't we?"

"Some of us are shattered beyond repair."

"There is no one beyond repair." Again the smile. I watched it soften the eyes, bring kindness to them.

"You need to go home," I said. "You don't belong here."

Antonio sighed. "No, no I do not. And yet here is where I find myself. Perhaps because there are words that you must hear."

"Me?" I felt another sliver of doubt about my safety and considered a grab for the sword.

"I am here for a reason, Natalee. Will you hear the words that are meant for you?"

I studied a display of spear points in a case across the room. He was clearly insane. Clearly.

"Yes," I whispered.

"You are loved, Natalee."

I nearly stood then, almost fled from the creepy words and the murky light and the strange man who whispered straight into my soul the words I most longed to hear.

But I stayed. Rooted to the black marble steps as though I were mounted there, my wounds on display for all to see.

"You are loved," he said again, and I fought against the tears that threatened.

"I was broken too, Natalee." He looked away, as though he studied a past too distant for memory. "Every day in the arena, facing a new foe. I fought and I killed, desperate for my own survival, yet hating my very existence." He nudged the sword that lay on the step between us. "I found myself in that arena as a consequence for violence, but the punishment only continued the violence, strengthened and hardened it until it was more a part of me than my heart or my lungs. Until it flowed through my veins and I breathed it like air." He turned his eyes on me, and I felt the strange weakness return. "There was no one more broken than I, Natalee. Not even you."

"You don't know what I've done. You can't say that."

"You have become a person you cannot approve."

"You've got that right."

"And yet, there is healing. There is restoration offered to you."

I sniffed. "I've been to counseling. They don't erase your past. They only tell you to ignore it, forget it."

"Learn from it."

"Yes, learn from it. And I've learned. I've learned that my mother was right. That I have no taste at all, not for beauty and not for men. And I've learned that married men lie, and that when their deceptions tear their lives apart, they run from everything and everyone that was part of their deception. And I've learned that when it's over, you are left alone and empty, and life is hollow and has no purpose!" I sat back against the marble step, wondering at my verbosity. My outburst had left me exhausted.

"Ah, Natalee." Antonio touched my arm. I resisted the urge to lean against his chest and weep.

Such a strange man.

"You have reached the very bottom, my child."

The tears did flow then, and I let them fall unhindered.

"Do you know there is one who has waited all your life for this moment?"

I turned to him. "I don't understand."

"I met him, you see. Not face-to-face but in the eyes and the hearts of those condemned to the arena as I was. Only these people went forth without sword, without helmet or shield." His voice and his face moved to that distant place again. I struggled to catch every quiet word.

"I had to kill them, Natalee. Can you imagine what this is like? To put a sword to someone whom you know is innocent and to know that you are the guilty one? And then one day as one young woman lay bleeding into the sand with the crowd on their feet roaring for me to end her life, I knelt and found redemption."

I searched his face, willed him to turn it back to me so I could find the answer there. "Tell me."

"Jesus. The woman spoke the name of Jesus, as though her life would not end in moments. She spoke the name into my eyes, into my heart, and I knew the truth."

I waited, hardly daring to breathe. He turned back to me, pleading with his own eyes for me to understand, trying to pass the truth to the next broken soul.

"She lived for the truth, and she died for it, Natalee. They all did. For one man who hung on a Roman cross for the sins of us all. Who paid the price to satisfy the judgment of God on our behalf. Who lived and died so that we could be made whole." Tears came to his eyes and flowed down cheeks that seemed to age before me.

"I held her in my arms, there in the sand. The crowd chanted again for me to put her to the sword, but instead I bent my head to her lips and heard her bless me." His voice caught. "She blessed me with the name of Jesus, the great healer of souls. The one who loved us all enough to die, and who lives again to restore us all to beauty."

I did fall against him then. In spite of myself, I buried my face in his chest and cried out the years of guilt, yet still unwilling to believe that this was truth.

"Natalee," Antonio pushed me away slightly, held my arms and looked in my eyes. "This is the message I came to bring you. There is one who sees all you have ever done, and loves you still. Loves you beyond human love, to the place of healing. His pain, his death—it pays the price for your past. Not erased. Not ignored. Redeemed, Natalee! Redeemed!"

My sobs had shortened to occasional sniffles now, and I wiped away the tears, wanting to believe. But it was all too strange, this encounter with Antonio. Too hard to believe a message had been brought to me on a lonely Christmas Eve.

Antonio picked up his sword and retrieved his helmet as if aware that his time with me must come to an end. And in that moment the door at the end of the Etruscan hall opened.

I looked up with resentment, unwilling to let go of the peace that had begun to fall over me.

A tall man in his forties stood at the doors, his hands on his hips.

"Antonio? What in the world are you doing?"

Antonio rose beside me, breathing deeply.

The man across the hall seemed to notice me for the first time. "Who are you?"

I stood beside Antonio. "Natalee Whitcombe. I work here. I restore pottery."

He took several determined steps toward us, and I saw that he wore dark-blue uniform pants, and a light-blue shirt with "Ted" stitched across the pocket.

"Shouldn't you have gone home by now?" Ted asked.

"Yes, I—I was just checking on something …"

I turned to Antonio, my excuse dying on my lips. He had removed the robe, and now was pulling the white tunic off, revealing an identical blue uniform beneath, complete with Antonio stitched on the shirt in dark-blue thread.

"Listen, Antonio," Ted was saying, "I know you're a history buff, but I've had about enough of your wandering the museum instead of doing your job."

Antonio nodded mutely beside me.

"He wasn't bothering you, was he, miss?" Ted asked me.

"Bothering me? No. No, he was—he was fine." I put a hand out to grasp the brass rail at the edge of the steps where we stood.

"Get the costume back to the Children's Room, Antonio. And then meet me in the Lower Egypt Hall. We need to get the mopping done before midnight."

Antonio bundled the robe and tunic in his hands, then picked up the artifacts and moved away without a glance at me. Ted seemed not to notice the treasures in Antonio's hands, and I assumed the older man would replace them in their glass exhibit before moving out of the Roman hall. He disappeared through the doors, leaving me alone and desolate with Ted.

"I'm really sorry about Antonio, miss. He's a bit past his prime, obviously, but he does good work around here. I occasionally find him playing dress-up, but he hasn't caused any real harm yet. I hope he didn't frighten you."

"No," I said. "I'm fine." The words mocked me, and I wondered if I'd ever be fine again. I felt like one who had jumped from a sinking ship to a lifeboat, only to discover that the lifeboat was ill patched and leaking.

"Let me walk you out, miss," Ted said, motioning toward the doors. I walked ahead of him as though in my sleep. In the Roman hall I gave a glance to the piece I'd come here to see, a symbol of the restoration I'd wished I could find for myself. The display case was too dark to see anything at all.

Through Rome, through Mesopotamia, through the remnants of my own broken life we walked until we reached the stairs.

"I'll be fine from here," I told Ted, anxious to be alone again. "I just need to get something from my office and then I'll head out.

Ted nodded. "Merry Christmas then."

I smiled. "Merry Christmas."

Outside my workroom, I fumbled with my key until it slid into the lock. I took one last look at the room, to be sure I'd left it in order. I wouldn't be coming back.

I lingered along the walk to the street exit, but minutes later the massive door sealed shut behind me and I stood alone in the cold.

"Natalee."

I turned to the now-familiar voice.

"Antonio." He wore only his maintenance uniform now, and his hands rested empty at his sides.

I didn't know what to say. He had deceived me completely, lured me into his dementia and given me false hope, yet I couldn't be angry at a feeble mind, heavy with kindness.

He took a step toward me, reached out his hand. "Things are not always what they seem."

I smiled, a tired smile with little left to give. "That's the truth."

Antonio stepped beside me and touched my arm with his hand. It was warm and rough, the callused hand of a janitor. Or a warrior. He pointed across the street, to the plaster nativity scene on the grassy lawn of the New City Church. I looked at the spotlighted manger.

Antonio whispered beside me. "Sometimes the glorious and the true comes disguised as the plain and humble."

I looked back to him, and he was gone. Not returned to the building. Not walking down the museum steps. I tell you truly, he was simply gone. A tingle went up my arm from the place where his hand had touched me, a current that seemed to find its way into my very soul. And I knew the truth.

And across the street the bells of the New City Church began to chime.

> "Hark! The herald angels sing,
> Glory to the newborn King!
> Peace on earth and mercy mild,
> God and sinners reconciled …"

ANGELA ELWELL HUNT

POINSETTIA PARABLE

ANDELINA RODRIGUEZ WAS BORN on the twenty-sixth day of December, an almost-Christmas birthday. Though some people might think a birthday during the holidays is another wonderful reason to make merry, Andelina thought her after-Christmas birthday was about as much fun as watching trees grow. Many of her presents were wrapped in leftover red and green foil, and her friends never wanted to come to her birthday parties because they were too busy playing with their Christmas toys.

Andelina's parents did their best to make her birthday seem like everyone else's. They decorated the house with bright blue and pink balloons, and her mother always baked an ordinary birthday cake. Her father made certain that his gifts were never, ever wrapped in red or green foil.

Aunt Dominga seemed to understand too. Though she lived far away in Mexico, she always sent Andelina a beautiful birthstone for her birthday: one year a ring, the next year a bracelet, the next a necklace. Andelina's birthstone was icy blue, as delicate as a diamond, and Aunt Dominga's note always said, "For my wonderful niece, the special December stone for a special December child."

But when the doorbell rang on Andelina's tenth birthday, she opened the door to discover a florist holding a large poinsettia plant. The attached card said, "For my wonderful niece: the special December flower for a special December child."

A poinsettia? That was a Christmas flower! Andelina carried the plant inside and set it on the floor next to the drooping Christmas tree. She tried to swallow the lump that rose in her throat. Aunt Dominga didn't understand at all.

December passed, and the Christmas decorations were

put away. Andelina took the poinsettia outside and left it on the back porch. The bright red leaves curled and fell off, and soon nothing remained but a stalk.

"You should take care of your plant," her mother told her. "It's a living thing, you know."

"It has sun and water," Andelina said. "It's okay."

But that spring, as the little poinsettia grew full and bright with green, Andelina's mother became very sick. She had to stay in bed all the time, so Aunt Dominga came from Mexico to help. "*Hola*, little one," she said, pressing her cheek to Andelina's after she had brought her suitcases into the house. "And how is my special niece?"

"OK, I guess," Andelina answered.

"You are so big!" Aunt Dominga knelt in front of Andelina. "I hope the plant I sent you is growing too. The poinsettias in Mexico grow to be ten feet tall!"

"It's growing," Andelina said, not really caring how tall a poinsettia could get.

Spring warmed into summer. Andelina's mother did not get better, so Aunt Dominga took over the running of the house. She cooked the meals, cleaned the floors, and tended the garden. Often Andelina saw her aunt fussing over the poinsettia on the back porch. She kept the stalks trimmed and the soil moist, but Andelina didn't care.

As the autumn leaves began to toast golden brown and fall from the trees, Andelina's mother had to go to the hospital. She was very sick, Aunt Dominga explained, and no one knew when she would come home again.

Leaving her aunt in the house, Andelina went to the back porch and sat down on a bench. She felt like there were tiny hands wringing her heart, squeezing hard until there was almost no feeling left. She lifted her eyes and saw the poinsettia she had ignored, now lush and green. How could it be so pretty, so healthy, when her mother was not?

"I hate you!" Andelina said. "You're not alive; you're just a dumb weed!"

Gathering all her strength, Andelina lifted the plant. She carried it toward the woods behind her house, swaying from side to side as she struggled under the weight of the heavy pot. She found a dark spot under the evergreen, shaded from the life-giving sun. Andelina didn't care if the plant died, and she didn't want Aunt Dominga around. She wanted her mother.

All through October, November, and early December, Aunt Dominga saw Andelina off to school in the morning and then went to the hospital. Alone at home in the afternoons, Andelina did her homework and chores and then sat by the front window. Christmas was coming, but no one in their family had time for candy canes or parties or decorating. They were too busy praying for her mother.

On Christmas Eve Andelina's father called and said that she must pray very hard, for her mother was weaker than she had ever been. Andelina fell to her knees and cried, begging God for help.

A soft touch woke her the next morning. Aunt Dominga's hand was on Andelina's shoulder, shaking her gently. "Merry Christmas, child," she said, sinking to the floor where Andelina had fallen asleep. "God has answered our prayers. Your mother is better."

"Oh, I'm so glad!" Andelina cried, throwing her arms about her aunt's shoulders. "And I'm so sorry, Auntie. I was angry; I wanted you to leave. I even tried to kill the poinsettia you sent me."

Aunt Dominga's hand stopped stroking Andelina's hair. "I wondered where it had gone."

Andelina wiped tears from her eyes. "I hid it in the woods. Deep under the trees."

Aunt Dominga's eyes brightened. "Come, child." She held out her hand. "Show me."

Andelina led her aunt into the woods. She had done a wicked thing. All plants needed sunlight to live, and the poinsettia would be ruined.

When Andelina found the shady spot deep among the trees, she gasped. The poinsettia sat there still, but it looked nothing like it had when she left it. The leaves that had been spindly and green were now as bright as a spill of crimson velvet over an emerald carpet.

She stared at the lovely flowers. "I thought it would die."

Aunt Dominga's arms slipped around Andelina's shoulders. "The poinsettia is a special plant. It needs long hours of dark to develop its pretty red leaves. If you had left it near the lights of the house, it would still be plain and green."

Carefully she turned Andelina, then stooped to look into the girl's eyes. "You are as special as that poinsettia, child, and one day soon you will bloom just as beautifully. When you pass through long months of darkness and waiting, you can have peace, knowing you are in the hands of the Master Gardener."

Aunt Dominga's dark eyes softened as she looked at the exquisite plant. "It is fitting that we should find this today, at Christmas, for the world was dark and waiting when Jesus was born to bring us hope and light. That's why the poinsettia is the December flower."

Aunt Dominga and Andelina carried the plant back to the house. When they reached the porch, they placed the poinsettia in a spot where everyone could see its splash of vivid color from inside the kitchen window.

As darkness drew down over the twinkling lights of the neighborhood, Andelina's father came home, a smile on his tired face. He hugged his daughter, wished her a merry Christmas, and said that her mother would soon be home.

"And I," Aunt Dominga said, "had better make plans for

the birthday cake I will bake tomorrow. What sort of cake would you like, Andelina?"

"I think," Andelina said, smiling as she looked out the window at the bright blooms, "that I'd like a different kind of birthday cake this year. A white one, decorated with red poinsettias."

MIKE NAPPA

MARY

"DO YOU LOVE ME?"

She spoke the words softly, but her eyes never loosed their hold on mine. Her eyes ... eyes that could tame anyone, anything. Deep, rich, chocolate brown eyes; round and full, with golden flecks hidden behind them and hints of secrets yet to come. Wonderful secrets, sorrowful secrets. Eyes so deep ... aaah, but I said that already.

She did not speak after the question. It seemed urgent, yet she refused to rush this moment. I rolled the words around in my head as I considered them. *Do you love me?* Did I love her? I was to marry her, of course, but did I love her?

She reached her hand out toward mine, and suddenly I was embarrassed for my fingers. My rough, scarred, calloused hands didn't deserve her gentle touch.

So young, she seemed so young right then. Almost as if she were a child reaching out to hold my hand as we walked together on some errand for nails or wood or food from the market.

Do you love me?

I wanted to say yes. She deserved a man who would say yes. And yet …

"I will learn to love you," I said finally. "And you will learn to love me."

Her eyes never looked away, but in the deepness behind them I watched a flickering gold flame extinguish itself. I'd never seen her eyes so flat, her face such stone. She managed a small smile, nodded, and gently pulled her hands away from mine.

"Yes," she said. "Perhaps."

So uncomfortable! How is it that this little woman, this almost-child could bring out such unease within me? I'd faced men a dozen times more terrible at my carpenter shop each day! I'd never backed down from anyone, not even my own father (may God rest his soul), not once I'd become a man. I saw the looks the young mothers gave me, heard them whisper to their children when they walked by, "There, see? Look at him. God be praised if you grow up to be a fine, honest carpenter like him."

And yet this woman, my soon-to-be wife, left me trembling with just a look.

O Mary, I thought, *why is your soul so downcast? What terrible burden have you come to bear that demands my love? My trust?*

All in good time, I decided. All in good time.

So, like the fool I was, I cleared my throat. "Well then. Is that it? Is that all you wanted to see me about?"

I stood to leave, thoughts already turning to the unfinished table and bench I was making for Rabbi Yeshva. He would be pleased when I finished it four full days early. And when Rabbi Yeshva was pleased, he was also generous.

"Joseph." Her back was turned to me, her voice so calm, so pale. So cold? I stopped midstride, staring at the slender shoulders and bowed head. Tracing the path of her elegant locks of midnight black hair as it cascaded forgetfully down her spine. Even from behind she was a beauty, better suited for a queen's purple robe than she was for that poor, tanned cloth that made up her dress. And ...

Was she trembling?

I waited, and then the words came, spilling from her lips into my ears like arrows from an archer's bow.

"Joseph," she said. "I'm pregnant. I'm to bear a baby, a special baby. The Son of God."

I know she turned to look at me then, but I did not see her. My eyes were filled with the sight of her in the act of love, forced to perform in the arms of one of those dirty, brutish, godless Romans. A soldier perhaps. Or a so-called nobleman. Evil men, really, no matter what they called themselves.

The hatred came quickly, filling me from the inside, threatening to spill out its venom directly on her. Then, just as quickly it faded, replaced now by an unquenchable sorrow, like a hunger that gnaws at the belly but is never satisfied.

And now I saw her, tears in her eyes, looking at me, searching. Desperately seeking what? Love? It was not possible; love was not what I had left to give.

I didn't speak. I did what only I could do at that moment. I turned and walked away. I felt her hand reach out and brush against my shoulder, but she didn't cry out. Moments later, I knew she would not follow.

"Rabbi Yeshva shall have his table today," I muttered through gritted teeth. "And tomorrow I shall be a richer man."

Yet, in spite of it all, I could feel nothing but poverty as I walked, no marched, from Mary's home to my workhouse.

Eloi, Eloi, lama sabachthani? my heart cried out in prayer. My God, My God, why have you forsaken me?

○◿

It was well into the night before I finished Rabbi Yeshva's table. For some reason my wood would not work as it was supposed to work. One leg of the table split right in half; a scratch marred another. And the bench seemed altogether too wet, wet with my tears.

It must have been only a few hours from morning when I finally was done with the cursed task. I looked over my work. Yes, in spite of the trials, the table was good and the bench even better. My bed held no attraction for me, so I sat on that bench and leaned on the table. It was time finally to think about my Mary, my betrothed, one who had been taken by another for some opportunistic satisfaction.

Poor Mary, I thought. She must have been frightened to make up such a mad story as she did. What was it she had said? "I'm to bear a baby, a special baby. The Son of God."

I snorted out loud, in spite of myself. The Son of God, yes? Perhaps the Messiah, our long-awaited savior? Yes, wouldn't that be poetic, the illegitimate son of a Roman soldier who grows up to be the Lord of Israel's revolution. *But I am no poet,* I thought. *Only a man no longer with a wife.*

I closed my eyes; it was her eyes I saw. I would put her away quietly, I decided. She could move to another town; no one would ever know. That would spare her life at least when there is no reprieve for our hearts.

"Joseph."

My eyes flew open. I jumped up from the bench, ready to defend my property. But I saw no one.

"Who are you?" I shouted. "And how did you get in here?"

Silence.

"If it's money you want, you'll not find any here," I announced as I began looking into the shadowy darkness of my workroom. I picked up a hammer, just in case it might be needed.

"Joseph, son of David."

Again the voice rang out, as if right in my ear. I turned swiftly, striking out with the hammer, but no one was there. How did this voice know I was descended from King David? I sighed. What would King David think now, to know one of his line had become simply a poor, hardworking carpenter, listening to voices in the dark.

"Joseph."

I put down the hammer. A presence seemed to fill the room, and somehow I knew it was not going to harm me. I sat on the bench, waiting. Finally I spoke, quietly this time, "Who are you?"

In response a light burned within the shadows, easily eclipsing the candles within my shop, and then blowing them out completely. Out of the light came a man, larger, brighter, more man than any I'd seen—and yet, not quite a man at all.

I knew immediately it was a visit from God, or perhaps one of his messengers. I dropped to the ground, face pressed against the dusty floor of my room. "Who are you, Lord?" I whispered.

Without a word the creature stepped to my side, put his hands under my shoulders and gently lifted me up to face him. I could feel the power pulsing through his fingers and knew that, if he wished, he could easily fling me into the heavens or squash me like a bug on the floor. Now it was my turn to tremble.

And then he smiled. He leaned over, whispering words in my ears, and behind the words were the faint sounds of bells as if a great announcement was being made.

"Joseph, son of David," he said. "Do not be afraid to take Mary home as your wife, because what is conceived in her is from the Holy Spirit. She will give birth to a son, and you are to give him the name Jesus, because he will save his people from their sins."

She spoke the truth! My Mary spoke the truth, and I believed a lie. Oh, would to God that I could take back my actions of the day before!

The man/angel leaned back from my ear, placed a hand under my chin to lift my eyes toward his. He smiled, and in his eyes I saw that familiar golden glint of secrets not yet told, joys not yet given, sorrows not yet endured.

I blinked, and he was gone. I found myself no longer standing, but sitting, no, lying across the new table I had just created. My hammer lay undisturbed; my candles still burned through the darkness of the room.

Had it all been a dream? I closed my eyes and now could see only the eyes of my angel telling me God's words, "Do not be afraid …"

℘

It was just after the rooster crowed when I knocked on the door to Mary's home. Her father was not happy to see me so early in the morning, but after some complaining, brought his daughter to the door. The circles under her eyes told me she had not slept; the stains around the knees of her robe revealed she had not abandoned prayer.

She gazed steadily into my eyes, and now I met her look without hesitation. "Yes, Mary. Yes," I said. "Yes, I do love you."

She said nothing, simply continued to stare deeply in my eyes. Was she looking for something there?

Say something, do something! I fretted to myself. Can't you see how much I need you? Isn't it obvious how I've always loved you? And I've only just now realized it … too late? Oh, Mary.… Please … God …

Deep in the recesses of my beloved's ebony eyes, a light flickered and came to life. She left out a soft sigh. And then my Mary smiled …

JANICE THOMPSON

CHRISTMAS AT THE CROSSROADS

HOUSTON, 1910

With one hand Maricella Alvarez clutched her beloved husband's letter to her breast. With the other she attempted to brush loose tears from her cheeks. Why she bothered she couldn't say. Certainly, no one could see her here in this dreary little boarding house, so far from the one she loved.

"Joseph, Joseph." She rocked back and forth in an attempt to bring comfort, but her aching heart wouldn't be silenced. Not yet. Not with the news so fresh.

Her tears tumbled down onto the page, smearing his carefully chosen words—so neat, so tidy, as always. She read them over again to be sure she hadn't misunderstood. Even through the smudges, the truth rang clear.

At that moment, the baby stirred within her, and Maricella jolted. The letter slipped from her hand and took flight, tipping this way and that in midair. Its slow and unpredictable movement held her captive and reminded Mari of her own life—as least thus far.

Had she not left her precious family in Laredo when her husband's railroad employment led them to Houston? Had she not transitioned from her familiar Spanish tongue to English, in an attempt to blend in upon arrival? And had she not silenced her fears as Joseph traveled up and down the line from Houston to Dallas, often leaving for weeks on end?

Yes, she had surely endured it all—and with little complaint. But this she couldn't bear. Not coming home for Christmas? Impossible. Not with their firstborn just weeks from arrival.

Maricella ran an open palm over her expanded midsection, tears coursing. "Joseph, you promised."

As she whispered the words, shame flooded her soul. How could she blame her husband when he worked so hard?

And clearly, judging from his carefully penned words, his disappointment greatly exceeded her own.

"*No es justo.*" It's not fair. She struggled as she reached down to pick up the letter, her ever-widening girth presenting a growing dilemma.

A rap at the door interrupted her thoughts. "Mrs. Alvarez?"

Mari wiped the dampness from her cheeks, knowing full well the persistent Mrs. Everson would not let up until she responded. She forced her voice to sound as normal as possible. "Yes?"

"Dinnertime." The woman's brusque voice had an authoritative ring to it. "No point in staying holed up in this room any longer. Not when I've got an excellent meal prepared downstairs." The motherly boarding house owner paused, as if to define her next words. "You need the nourishment, my dear. And the baby does as well."

Maricella dabbed the moisture from her nose with a handkerchief and gave a little sniffle. "I'll be down shortly."

"We'll not say grace until you come."

The click of Mrs. Everson's high-button shoes against the wooden stairs stirred something in Maricella. "I should go down to dinner," she whispered. "It will do me good."

She went to the dressing mirror and pressed a bit of powder on the tip of her shiny pink nose. As she gave her eyes one last swipe with the hankie, Mari stared at her somber reflection. How could Joseph consider her his "little Spanish beauty" now, when she looked so miserable?

She made her way down the stairs to the large dining room. Familiar faces lined each side of the table. Elderly Mr. Jenkins, who stayed in the room across from hers, gave a polite nod. Mrs. Overstreet, a young widow, seemed distracted with scolding her two little boys and didn't seem to notice she'd entered the room. Ida Nordstrom, the shy schoolmarm, flashed a silent smile. And Mrs. Everson greeted Maricella with the gusto due an approaching royalty.

"Ah, my dear! You've graced us with your presence as I knew you would. Must've been the smell of my pot roast and potatoes, eh?"

Maricella forced a smile as she sat. "Yes'm." In truth, the food smelled heavenly.

They bowed their heads and Mr. Jenkins led them in a heartfelt prayer. Mari listened to his words but could scarcely understand their depth. How could this loving God of whom he spoke separate a man from his wife and child, particularly in a season such as this?

The clinking of knives and forks replaced her lingering questions, and Mari ate as if she might never have the opportunity to do so again. At some point along the way, she found herself distracted by the decorations Mrs. Everson had placed about the room. Bright red napkins lined each spot at the table. A colorful Christmas wreath hung above the stone fireplace. Swags of greenery wrapped the stair railing and a sprig of mistletoe hung above the doorway nearby.

Somehow she couldn't get beyond the mistletoe.

After dinner, Mari revisited her room and her situation. Perhaps a decent night's sleep would do her good. Surely everything would look better in the morning. And perhaps Mr. Jenkins' God would see fit to perform the miracle she longed for.

She wrestled with the bed sheets for hours, wondering if the ache in her heart would ever dissipate. A seemingly impossible idea presented itself somewhere between the hours of 2:00 and 3:00 in the morning and she could not let it go.

If Joseph couldn't come to her for Christmas, then perhaps—just perhaps—she and the baby could go to him.

The idea grew like a seed firmly planted in Maricella's mind. She fell into a fitful sleep sometime before 4:00, and a rap on the door awakened her just three hours later.

"Breakfast, Mrs. Alvarez. You need to keep up your strength."

The thought of food offered a temptation, to be sure, but another plan, far superior to eating, gave her cause to reconsider. Maricella slipped out of her nightgown and dressed in clothing suited to traveling, then quickly put together a little bag of personal belongings. "Just enough for a week or so."

She looked over the tiny room, hoping she hadn't forgotten

anything of consequence. "Ah, yes." She reached into the hand-carved jewelry box and pulled out the tiny roll of bills. "Wouldn't want to forget this."

Then, as if she had been planning this excursion for ages, Maricella tiptoed out of the room, down the stairs, beyond the bustling dining room, and out the front door.

Once outside, she shivered against the cold and the child inside stirred, finally awakened to the day's activities.

"Good morning, little one," Mari spoke aloud as she laid a hand against her belly. "We're going to see Papa." Just speaking the words aloud gave her courage.

She pulled her cloak taut about her shoulders and set out on her way. She caught the Harrisburg streetcar to the busy Houston train station, where, after a slight debate with the ticket master over the risks of traveling in her delicate condition, she purchased a ticket to Dallas. The train would leave promptly at 10:15, which left two hours to spare—two agonizing hours, contemplating the seeming foolishness of her decision.

Have I lost control of my senses? Should I turn around and go back home? The thought would not give her leave.

By the time the "all aboard" rang out, Maricella had very nearly changed her mind. However, something about the rumble of the train made her long for Joseph even more. With some assistance from the porter, she boarded the iron horse and sat in a section near the back—a car filled with squirming children, tired mothers, and a handful of folks who looked more like vagabonds than world travelers.

Resting against the back of the seat, Mari tilted her head to gaze out of the window. "Good-bye, Houston."

The train let out a piercing whistle, then jolted as they headed off on their way. Too late for misgivings. Too late for afterthoughts. From this point forth, Maricella would only think of one thing: what she would say to Joseph when they saw one another for the first time. She couldn't help but smile as she imagined the look on her precious husband's face when he saw her.

Immediately the smile faded. What if he scolded? Or worse. What if she couldn't locate him in Dallas and found herself completely alone?

Mari shivered. Best to push these thoughts from her mind. No point in worrying about the unknown.

As if on cue, the baby wrestled a bit within her and Maricella drew in a deep breath. Conviction set in right away. *What have I done? Have I put my child's life at risk? And for what—a foolish girl's whim? A fancy?*

Suddenly she longed for Houston, ached for the boarding house and the comfort of Mrs. Everson's tantalizing dinner table delights. She longed for the security of the midwife and the ever-present prayers of Mr. Jenkins. She missed her tiny room with its large four-poster bed and oversized wardrobe.

Maricella squeezed her eyes shut and tried to rest. For

hours the train chugged along, headed north on the same track that carried Joseph back and forth. She had often wondered what it might feel like to make this journey. Now she could speak from firsthand experience.

Outside her window the dry grasses of the Texas flatlands rolled by. They offered little to encourage the Christmas spirit. In fact, they seemed almost to mock it. Mari rested against the seat and allowed her thoughts to drift to the holiday. Childhood memories of Christmases spent sipping hot chocolate and nibbling at her mother's holiday sweets served to bring a smile to her lips. How many years had she gathered around the tree on Christmas morning with her seven brothers and sisters, singing *"Noche de paz, noche de amor."*

The little melody for "Silent Night" now wrapped her in its grip, and she hummed as the memories continued to flood over her. Other recollections surfaced as well. Perhaps, even more than singing, listening to her father read the Christmas story in his big, booming voice had brought the greatest comfort.

Funny, actually. His God sounded a lot like the one Mr. Jenkins spoke so highly of.

Mari contemplated the beliefs of the two men and wondered, even then, if she had done herself a disservice by so carefully avoiding the question of the Christ of Christmas. His tale of stables and hay seemed more the stuff of fairy tales. Hmm. Perhaps she would have time to dwell on it later.

Her eyes grew heavy as the thoughts faded, and she dozed until the woman in the seat across from her startled her awake with the words, "They're serving lunch."

Maricella made her way through the crowd of people to the dining car, where she waited some time for a place to sit. She eventually found herself seated across the table from a total stranger—a fellow with a shock of near-white blond hair.

"Pleased to make your acquaintance." He extended a hand. "Name's Gabe."

She nodded politely. "Maricella Alvarez."

"You're from the Valley."

"H … how did you know that?" She couldn't help but stare.

He shrugged. "Just guessing. To be honest, I've never been south of Houston, but I've acquired a knack for dialects."

Mari shook off her curiosity and turned her thoughts to food. She ordered a sandwich and a steaming bowl of vegetable soup. As she ate, Gabe rambled on and on, chattering about the holiday, the weather, the length of the trip, and the history of the railroad. She did all she could to tune him out.

As they finished, she thanked her dining partner for a lovely time and headed back to her seat. Once there, she settled back down to rest once more. Just as her eyes slipped shut, the child within began to stir. *Oh, not now,* bambino. *Mama's too tired to argue with you at the moment.* As if on command, the little one relented and grew still.

Mari took one last look out of the window before giving in to the exhaustion. An uneasy feeling gripped her stomach—a curious tightness. Surely she could benefit from a bit of sleep.

The grinding of brakes awakened her some time later, along with the raised voices of travelers seated nearby. Mari struggled to remember where she was. She turned to the woman sitting across from her. "W … what happened?"

At that moment the conductor made an appearance in the car. "Ladies and gentlemen, we've run into a bit of a problem. A section of track is out just north of here, and I'm afraid we're going to have to stop."

Stop? For how long?

He disappeared into the next car and Mari turned to her neighbor. "Where are we?"

"From my calculations, we're just a few miles shy of Centerville," the man to her left responded.

"Centerville?" She looked out of the window again, the late afternoon sun nearly blinding.

"It's about halfway between Houston and Dallas." The fellow yawned. "A scheduled stop. It's not a very large town, but there's a comfortable hotel. I'm sure the railroad will put us up for the night."

"Put us up in a hotel? On Christmas Eve?" Fear niggled at Maricella. *I've only made it halfway. I'll never get to Joseph by Christmas.* Indeed, her impulsive plan seemed destined to fail.

A half hour later, the conductor reappeared. "We'll be taking you in shifts to the hotel in Centerville—women and children first, men to follow."

With the sting of fresh tears in her eyes, Maricella made her way off of the train. She kept one hand on her belly, the other clutching her bag. As she stood in the middle of the field, she felt a presence at her side.

"Don't be afraid." A familiar male voice spoke.

She looked over to find Gabe standing beside her. His expression, peaceful and serene, lifted her spirits immediately. "Oh, I'm so glad to see you. I feel so …"

"Alone?" He spoke with authority and a sense of knowing.

A lone tear trickled down Mari's cheek. "Yes, alone. And so very foolish." She bowed her head and the tears fell.

"Nothing to feel foolish about," he assured her. "I'm sure you've a wonderful reason for being here."

A slight twisting in Maricella's belly distracted her momentarily. "I … I …"

"I'll stick by you till you're safely on the buggy. I don't want you out here amongst the people by yourself."

"Thank you." She rubbed a hand across her midsection, curious as to the sudden tension there. "I'm sure everything will be fine."

"Oh, it will be. Of that I can assure you." He flashed a confident smile, then took her by the arm and led her to the buggy. With an extended hand, he helped her up into the seat then gave her a curious look as she struggled with the ever-growing pain. "Are you not well?"

She bit her lip, unable to speak—at least for now. "I … I'm not sure. I'm feeling a bit …"

Gabe immediately snapped to attention. "Ah, I see. Well, I'll be coming along for the ride, then." He took charge of the situation immediately and boarded the buggy in the seat next to her. "My home is in Centerville. My wife will know what to do."

"B … but … the hotel?"

"The hotel will be filled with frustrated travelers, vying for rooms. That will never work for you. Besides, my Angela will know what's best," he explained. "And she's worked as a midwife before."

"Midwife?" Another pain gripped her middle and Maricella drew in a deep breath. "It's too soon for a midwife. The baby isn't due for another month."

"Yes, well …" His eyebrows raised as the horse-drawn buggy began to move. "We'll see about that."

Maricella found it difficult to focus as they barreled their way toward Centerville. When they reached the large home set in the middle of exquisite ranchland, she breathed a sigh of relief. *A hot bath and a good night's sleep and I'll be as good as new.*

At that very moment, another pain gripped her.

A lovely woman emerged from the house with a broad

smile on her face. Her white hair, swept up in a lovely comb seemed curiously out of place in such a rustic setting, and her cheeks glowed pink against the setting sun. Gabe's feet no sooner hit the ground than she wrapped him in a loving embrace. "Gabriel!"

"I've missed you, Angel," he said. "But I'm afraid we've got a visitor who needs your attention more than I do."

Angela looked up with compassionate eyes, and Maricella at once felt safe.

"Oh, my dear!" The older woman nodded, understanding fully. "Let's get you inside."

Mari exited the buggy as soon as the pain left. Angela led her into the beautiful home and through the doors of the front bedroom.

"Do you have a nightgown in that bag, dear?"

"I … I do." She fumbled to open the traveling case, but underneath her trembling hands it would not cooperate.

"Let me help you with that." Angela easily opened the bag then reached inside. "Now let's get you into something more comfortable."

Less than ten minutes later Mari sat in the bed, wrapped up in a down comforter with a cup of hot tea in her hands. The birthing pains came more consistently now. No denying the inevitable. Her long-awaited child would shortly enter the world.

Joseph fidgeted in his seat on the southbound train and glanced at his watch for the hundredth time: 6:11 p.m. To his right, the sun pressed itself beyond the horizon, casting an eerie orange glow across a near-dark sky. Within minutes, it would disappear altogether.

"Your pass, please, Joseph." Longtime friend and conductor Carter Winthorpe extended a hand.

Joseph pulled out his traveling pass—just one of the luxuries his employment provided. "Here you go."

The elderly man's thick handlebar moustache furrowed a bit as he punched a hole through the card. "Not often we see you as a passenger, eh?"

"No, and I can't say that I like it much." Joseph shook his head in frustration. "Are you sure you can't put me to work? I feel so useless sitting here."

"Nope." The conductor chuckled. "We've got all the brakemen we need on this run."

Joseph leaned back against the seat and contemplated his situation. Things certainly had a habit of not going as planned. When word came that he could leave the Dallas area, he'd been elated. With no time to contact Mari, he'd just have to surprise her.

But now, from what he'd just been told, a loose section of track about twenty minutes south might disrupt his plans. They would stop somewhere near the crossroads. And there they would remain until morning.

Christmas morning. A morning he'd planned to spend wrapped in Maricella's arms, kissing away the tears of the past two weeks.

Joseph cringed. "Lord, why?" Why on such a night as this when his hopes and plans seemed within his grasp?

The train came to a grinding halt just minutes north of Centerville. From here passengers would face two possibilities: either stay onboard till morning, or travel to town for a room at the hotel.

He opted for the second. Even in his exhausted state, the idea of sleeping in this seat didn't settle well.

Half an hour later Joseph found himself in the most crowded hotel lobby he'd ever seen. Babies cried, women scolded, and seedy-looking men hovered nearby, the stench of alcohol so strong on their breath that he could scarcely pass by without feeling ill.

He shrugged in the hotel clerk's direction. "No rooms?"

The exhausted fellow behind the desk shook his head. "I'm afraid not, sir. A spot in the lobby is about the best we can offer at this point. I'm so sorry."

I would have done better to stay on the train.

Joseph slid down on the floor and rested his aching back against the wall. He needed a soft bed, not this ridiculous inconvenience. Still, he settled in and tried to sleep, doing everything in his power not to think about Maricella.

A rush of cold air swept by as a man with white-blond hair

raced into the lobby. "Excuse me!" he paused to catch his breath. "I'm looking for someone who speaks Spanish."

The hotel clerk gave a shrug, and looked about. "Does anyone here speak Spanish? Habla espanole?"

Joseph chuckled at the fellow's poor attempt at the language, but his curiosity certainly kept his attention focused on the clerk. When no one else responded, he finally said, "I … I speak Spanish."

"Oh, praise God." The blond man clapped his hands together. "Would you mind coming with me? In exchange for your time, I can offer you a hot meal and a warm bed."

"Can't argue with that. Certainly sounds better than what I've got here." Joseph rose from his spot and followed the anxious gentleman to a car outside.

Where they were headed, he had no idea.

ଔ

"You're doing just fine, honey. Just fine."

Maricella gritted her teeth and bore down, the pressure too intense to speak. She gasped for breath and Angela wiped her brow with a damp cloth.

"Oh, *¡el dolor!*" The pain, the pain!

Try as she might, Mari couldn't make the words come out in English. Not now. She felt the usual urge to push and reached up to grip the headboard. "*No mas,*" she groaned. No more.

Angela approached the foot of the bed, eyes widening.

"We're getting close now. Won't be long."

At that moment, a flash of lights outside the window distracted Maricella.

"Oh, thank God," Angela exclaimed. "Gabe's home."

Mari bit her lip and fought to stay focused.

A rap sounded at the door and Gabe's loving voice rang out. "I've got someone here who speaks Spanish. What should we do? Should I send him in?"

"Him?" Mari's response came out in English, and she shook her head, near frantic. "No! Not a man. Not now."

Off in the distance, a clock chimed midnight. At that very moment, Maricella gave herself over to the delivery of the child. Nothing, no one could stop the process now. Moments later, her son made his entrance—and the whole room suddenly felt like Christmas.

"Oh, *mi hijo, ¡mi hijo*!" Oh, my little son!

Suddenly the door to the room burst open. Maricella lifted her eyes in terror. Who would interrupt such a private and sacred moment? The shadow of a man she knew quite well fell across the bed. "J … Joseph?"

"Mari!" Joseph's eyes filled with tears. "I knew your voice. I knew it." The weeping began in earnest now. "And when I heard the baby's cry …" He leaned his head into her arm, tears flowing.

Mari trembled in shock. "But how did you … how did you get here?"

"I don't know," he looked up with tear-stained eyes. "I truly don't. But I'm here. That's all that matters now."

She shook her head in disbelief.

Joseph gazed at his son in awe. "We'll call him Jacob, *sí?* After your father."

"Jacob. *Sí.*" She nodded then cradled the infant in her arms.

With a loving nod, Angela slipped out of the room, leaving them alone.

"It's Christmas," Joseph whispered.

A lump grew in Mari's throat. For some reason, her father's prayer rose to her memory once again and suddenly she understood, truly understood. *Oh, Lord, I see. In this child's eyes, I see.*

Outside the door, Gabe and Angela broke into song, their voices blended in angelic refrain. "Silent night, holy night" rang out across the house.

Maricella closed her eyes and drank in the wonder. With her baby nestled in her arms and her husband at her side, revelation came in steady waves.

This night, this holy Christmas night, she had not only witnessed a miracle …

She had truly participated in one.

JOHN DUCKWORTH

ANGELS WE HAVE HEARD ON HIGH

YOUNG PASTOR TORGENSON, RESPLENDENT in the new three-piece, charcoal gray suit his wife had given him especially for this Christmas Eve service, mounted the platform. An ocean of faces looked back at him—the faces of the Red Ridge Community Church, holiday-excited and ruddy from the cold outside.

The pastor smiled for a second at his wife, who beamed from the first row; then he began. "Before the choir sings our anthem, 'Angels We Have Heard on High,'" he said, "let me remind you of a Scripture passage about angels. Turn with me to Hebrews 13:2, if you will …"

A tissue-thin shuffle of Bible pages went through the sanctuary like a rushing wind. Then it stopped, and as the pastor was about to read Hebrews 13:2, a murmur rose in the rear pews near the door.

To the consternation of several older members, a shocking pair of visitors had entered. The man was tall, blond, bushy-bearded—a near skeleton in a grimy navy pea coat. The girl was very, very pregnant, swathed in a shapeless beige peasant dress and a tattered sweater. A kerchief failed to conceal her stringy black hair.

"Wonder if they're married?" whispered a woman in the back row.

"I never saw the like, not in this church," grumbled a man. From her usual seat, old Mizzie Everett just squinted at the strangers, apparently as confused as ever.

Pastor Torgenson paused, smelling trouble. *Another battle of the old and the new,* he sighed to himself. *Would it never end?*

"Welcome," he finally called out to the bedraggled strangers. "We're glad you're here. Sit right down."

But it was easier said than done. The young couple had to wind their way to the front to find the only vacant seats. A few hundred curious eyes watched.

"Now, as I was saying," the young preacher continued. "Hebrews 13:2." He cleared his throat. "Do not forget to entertain strangers, for by so doing some people have entertained angels without knowing it."

He gulped, surprised at the verse's sudden aptness. "Well. Uh, perhaps you've read stories about Christmas visitations by angels. Many have been written, most of them pure fiction. But let's remember tonight that our Lord himself was not recognized for who he was. And let's make sure there's room at our inn tonight." A nod to the choir and he sat down by the pulpit.

The music billowed behind him. He tried not to stare at the young couple but couldn't help it. Who were they? Why were they here?

All at once it hit him. On Christmas Eve, a bearded young man and a pregnant woman seeking shelter? Did they have a donkey parked outside too?

He smiled to himself. *Entertained angels without knowing it? Well, one never knew ...*

The choir's last "Gloria in excelsis deo" faded, and the pastor jumped to his feet. He had an idea.

"In our bulletin, the order of service calls next for a pastoral prayer. But before I lead us, let's find out what we have to pray about on this Christmas Eve. Jack ..." he motioned to an usher. "If you'll get the moveable microphone, we can have a brief time of sharing our needs."

Again, the pastor tried not to gaze at the young strangers but hoped they'd share their obvious needs. After all, this was a unique chance for the church to show hospitality, he thought.

"Just a brief time," he repeated, unconsciously nodding at old Mizzie Everett in the back. Poor old Mizzie, they called her. She loved sharing times. At the first click of the microphone, she'd jump up as quickly as her arthritis allowed, only to ramble on and on about some long-forgotten event or person. The whole congregation would look at the floor, embarrassed as Mizzie tried to remember a Bible verse or sing a song in her rusty squeal of a voice. It was starting to put a damper on services, some people said.

The pastor's hopes rose as the bearded young man started to get to his feet. But Mizzie was up first, and she took the microphone from the reluctant usher. An almost audible groan went up from the congregation.

"Uh, thank you, Mizzie," the pastor said after a minute of the old woman's rambling. But she droned on.

I wish she'd take a hint, the pastor thought. Poor old Mizzie—her mind's starting to go, and she still pedals that three-wheeled bicycle all over town, making a spectacle of herself. Even the older members shook their heads about it.

Finally she surrendered the microphone. "We'll be sure to pray about that, Mizzie," the pastor said and then looked down at the young couple. This time the skinny fellow made it all the way to his feet.

"I-I don't know anything about talkin' in church," he began shakily. "But my old lady …" he indicated the girl at his side. "… I mean, my, uh, wife and I really need a place to stay tonight. We saw the lights and came in."

The pastor watched the young man speak, touched by his need. "We're glad you did," the pastor said, "and I'm sure we can find you a place to stay. By the way, what's your name?"

The young man looked away shyly. "I'm Joe," he said, "and this is Mary."

A startled murmur was heard. "Joseph and Mary?" the pastor asked incredulously.

"Yeah, I know how it sounds," the young man said, growing red faced. "But it's true, really."

The pastor couldn't hold back a chuckle of wonderment. "Indeed it is," he said and quoted Hebrews 13:2 again. Inspired, he thanked the young man and prayed fervently for the couple's needs, for the families gathered there, and the war-weary world's longing for peace on earth.

There was no doubt about it—the choir sounded sweeter than ever that night. The ancient story from Luke was never better read nor more poignant. Even the atmosphere seemed rare, closer to heaven, with the young couple sitting there in the front. When the time had come for the benediction, Pastor Torgenson looked out on the Christmas Eve faces and spoke from his heart.

"Let there be room in our inn tonight," he said. "Let us reach out to the Lord of Christmas and to one another. We may be different, but because he came we can be one."

Downstairs, where the church ladies had prepared punch, coffee, and cookies, the congregation streamed in for a bit of fellowship. The pastor and his wife brought cups of coffee to the young man and woman, only to discover that several parishioners had already done the same.

"We'd be happy to have you stay at our house tonight, Joe and Mary," volunteered a middle-aged couple.

"We were going to say the same thing," said two others. A group of high schoolers brought cookies and punch to the strangers. Pastor Torgenson, smiling broadly, hugged his wife.

Over in the corner by the coffee percolator, old Mizzie Everett sat alone, with both hands around a cup of punch. She squinted at the sea of people, seeming confused by the noise.

Suddenly she put down her punch and looked at her watch. As if on schedule, she picked up her purse and made her way to the door along the crowd's edge. Nobody noticed her leave.

The night was cold. Setting her jaw determinedly, Mizzie struggled against her arthritis to mount her three-wheeled bicycle.

So frail, these mortal bones, she thought, dumping her purse in the bike's basket. Her legs strained, pumping the pedals. Iced puddles cracked under her wheels all the way out of town.

The city-limits sign flashed past. Wheezing, she knew she could go no further. Finally she slowed and parked by the side of the road.

The highway was deserted. Only the stars and heaven watched as she climbed the sloping field by the road, her breath coming in hoarse gasps. A dog barked in the distance.

Christmas Eve, she thought, looking at the sky. Just like that first Christmas Eve, when she had sung with the others. Oh, but that had been easy compared with this assignment. This time she'd had to take on a body for such a long time. Not like the Sodom and Gomorrah visit or the rest.

She stretched and felt a pain. It was good to be going home.

Smiling, she closed her eyes and reached heavenward. Slowly the creases in her face vanished, and the twisted hands unfurled. *Going home,* she thought.

Brighter and brighter her face glowed, her old coat transformed into a robe the color of the sun. It was an angel's robe.

At last, she thought, *at last.* There was a silent flash in the night, and Mizzie Everett was gone.

STRIKE

JEFFERSON TURNER STRODE DOWN the dark dirt road quickly, but not serenely, coming to the door of his cabin. Overhead, the bright stars, the silvery winter moon, the generosity of the night sky, gentle guides to his nocturnal journey, offered no comfort. Oblique to his affection for Emily was the notion that he could go no further with her. If he pursued what had begun as an innocuous friendship but had now turned so passionate, he feared it would not end well for either of them. And there was nothing worse a man could do than to let a woman down when the bar of expectation had been raised so high. Where could their passion lead? He tried to envision such a destination through the fog of his thinking—to a surreptitious wedding, to marriage and children, to an old age spent together in a bliss rummaged from memories of courtship, because that was all they had in common. What about when the feelings burned low, leaving mere embers with their somber glow? When Emily saw him and his life in the clear light of the unvarnished day, the way the townspeople saw him, the way, surely, her father saw him, would she feel the same?

He hit the wooden planks of his cabin door with the butt of his fist. It swung wide slamming against the wall. Shaking off the chill air, he slammed the door and bolted it, then struck a blue tip against his rugged table. The flame licked the kerosene-soaked wick of his lantern, fanning its dim aura into the rustic cabin.

Across the room, next to his bunk in a corner the light hardly touched, he thought he saw a figure sitting upright with a full dress outlined in degrees of shadow. He sighed and looked away. Even the eyes of his mind conspired against him in their complicit effort to make him want her. The memory of the deep blueness of her dress reflecting the kind azure of her eyes, tandem workers against his rational mind, would probably never fade. But it would have to. He didn't intend to see her again. He lit the kindling in the stove, feeding in a few white faced slabs of pine, watching them catch, snapping, popping. Rubbing his hands together, he turned. In the fullness of the light the figure in the corner came clearly into view.

"What … what are you doing here?"

"You left in such a hurry, you forgot your gift." She didn't move from her seat.

"You shouldn't have come." He did not approach her.

"Why," she said. "Because it's not proper? Or because you didn't want me to see where you live?"

He gave his attention to the fire, his back to her, thrusting in a larger log. He didn't want to dignify her questions with answers. There were no answers, only the truth.

"Please take it," she said with a plaintive voice he could not long turn his back to, but he continued to stare into the bristling flame. He imagined her holding out her gift to him, an emerald birth stone set in gold on the left middle finger of her slender ivory-colored hand.

"I can't take anything else from you."

"Have you taken so much from me you can't stand me?"

He smirked, the heat rising on his face as he squatted low, perpendicular to the flames. "You don't know me."

"Jefferson …"

His name from her mouth quickened his soul. When he could take it no longer, he swiveled on the balls of his feet, his boots scrunching on the dusty planks.

"Jefferson." She leaned forward, long dark curls falling across her face. "I do know you, that's why I came."

He glared hard at her. From the moment he saw her last year coming out of the mercantile on State Street he couldn't get her off his mind. Now she sat across from him in the half-light, smelling of lavender and lilies and he wanted to hold her hand, to touch her long, curly black hair … but he had to put her out of his mind. He hadn't come to San Francisco to find a wife but to find his fortune. Even then what did he have to offer her, empty holes from his claim up the Sacramento? He must harden himself against the beauty of her eyes, the wonder of her smile, the cordiality of her laugh. He had come to San Francisco to find gold, to pay off his family's debts, to solve a problem, not create another one.

"Why did you leave the party so abruptly? Is there something here," she waved her empty hand at the sparse room, "that's so pressing you had to leave before I could give you your gift?"

"I think the only reason your father allowed you to invite me was so he could embarrass me."

"My father meant no harm."

"There are many ways to harm a man, Emily."

"And a woman," her voice dropping. "He simply asked you about your father."

"He knows more about my father than I do. He only asked it so the whole room could hear it. All of Nob Hill was in your parlor."

"Indeed," she said, a sparkle in her voice. "It was a lovely Christmas celebration."

"Emily …"

"You've been calling on me for the past eight months," she interrupted him. "Why do you think my father wouldn't ask about your past?"

"I've told you everything," he said, stripping the emotion out of his voice.

"Everything?"

The firelight reflected off her blue silk dress, while a hint of light danced in her eyes. She sat demurely, the gift in her lap.

"Yes, of course I've told you everything," he said in a clipped tone. "You know my father died when his print shop burned down around him. That I had no choice but to drop out of Princeton in my third year, that my family is deeply in debt because of my father's business. And that I borrowed from my mother's last bit of money to stake me here in California. I have to pay her back or she'll be living on the street soon. And now we need to be truthful with each other. You and I are so different. All I have to offer is the life of a miner, not even a successful one."

"And you're thinking all of that would change if you could just make your strike."

"Isn't that what you're expecting too?"

She thought for a moment. "You didn't come straight here after you left our house."

"I went to the Charles Hotel."

"To distract yourself from what you see as your misfortune," she said

"It's Christmas Eve; they only served sarsaparilla."

"If you wanted a drink, you should have stayed for the wassail."

He swiveled back around, facing the fire. "You know it's not to be between us."

"Who said I came here to talk about us."

"Then what have you come here for?"

"Your gift, you left without it." Again he sensed that she held it out to him, willing him to take it.

He rubbed his clean-shaven chin as he fixed on the flame. If he took the gift, he would be indebted to her,

letting her think he would reciprocate, and he had neither the resources nor the time for that. He'd already had
to sell his horse. His mine, his claim, his work up in the
hills consumed him. It was all he had now. That was why
he had come to California, wasn't it? But if he did take
the gift, then he could be rid of her quickly and then it
would be up to him to avoid her. That would not be easy,
but it was possible. He would send Harley to town for
supplies; he would mend his own clothes instead of taking them to the Chinese laundress. He could easily
outwit her if he tried.

"Why is it that men are so predictable?"

He half turned his head. "Is that how you see me?"

"If you take the gift, you're thinking you'll owe me.
I'm celebrating a tradition of giving and you're thinking
of how you can repay me."

"When is Henry coming back to pick you up?"

"Now, you see, you're considering taking the gift if it
means I'll leave and be out of your life."

"Your father will find out where you went tonight.
Then he'll run me off my claim."

"You think ill of him."

"I can see it in his eyes; he scrutinizes me like he sifts
wheat."

"The fire only hurts if it has something to burn."

"Don't be naive. We all have something to burn."

"Maybe so," she said softly.

"I'm sorry, I should have never kissed you."

"But I kissed you."

"Is that why you're here?"

"No ..."

The fire in the stove burned hotter, blanching his face, but he didn't move.

"Actually, this is from ... my father," she said. Again, she held out her hand, this time stiffly, across the long divide between them.

He stood and shucked off his coat—his one good coat—and loosened the collar of his shirt. His mother had given him a new suit before he left Philadelphia. She had fought back tears when he left, but what choice did he have? He had hefted the clothes, with all of his other supplies, across the wide and wild continent to his new home. He would need it when he reached civilized society, she had told him. Society sat across from him, and he didn't feel like he fit in anymore. Gifts, parties, decorations, family, he had given it all up to seek his fortune. He donned his buffalo-skin jacket and thought about all the digging he could get done tomorrow. He had been digging for two years with miserable results; he would dig for the next ten years if that's what it took.

"I don't understand this," he said. "The streets of San Francisco are filled with thieves who have more gold dust in their pockets than I've pulled out of the earth in the last two years."

"You don't believe anymore, do you?"

He shook his head and turned away from her. "I'm having a hard time believing."

"I remember once you quoted something to me, 'Ask, and it shall be given you, seek and ye shall find.'"

"I'm having a harder time with that one."

"Jefferson, sometimes answers come from directions we're not expecting. But answers do come. Please take it." She stretched out her hand again.

He turned to her. "So, why would your father give this to me?" His voice was sharp, as he faced her, hands on his hips, and nodded toward the little package in her outstretched hand. It was wrapped in a blue cloth, the excess tied in a bundle at the top with a blue silk ribbon.

"Like you said, he's sifted you ..."

Jefferson looked it over. It lay in the palm of her hand. It wasn't anything he could use on his claim, certainly not one of those steam-driven contraptions that ripped the earth up tons at a time like those Belloti brothers had up river. No wonder they were wealthy. The gift was as small and diminutive as his dreams were becoming.

Jefferson pursed his lips, folded his arms across his chest.

"Henry will be here soon," an urgency to her voice. "Are you going to take it?"

"It's not from you?"

She shook her head, her hand flat, steady, the blue cloth wrapped tight in the center of her palm.

"Is it something I can use?"

"You may visit us the next time we play charades, but usually people don't play that game with a gift." She wasn't smiling anymore.

What did it matter? She wasn't going to leave without him taking it. He took one step, two steps forward, reached out, snatching it up quickly. He weighed it in his hand. It couldn't weigh more than a pound. A trinket. Something to mock him.

"Usually people open their presents and smile even if they don't like it."

"Yes they do," he said a little sarcastically.

Here she lived in the untamed hills of San Francisco in the midst of a tumultuous gold rush where men ruthlessly jumped claims with impunity, killed each other over the most trivial accusations, and she was concerned with maintaining niceties? But there was no reason to insult her. She had come all the way out here to deliver a gift. He held his tongue and stripped off the ribbon. In the midst of the blue cloth lay a rock. What kind of rock?

He took it to the fire. As he stared wide-eyed at the

glinting piece in the palm of his hand, he heard the jingle of bridles and the snort of horses outside his door.

"That's Henry." She rose and crossed to the door, her silk dress rustling, rushing past him while he stared at the rock in his hand.

"Is this some kind of joke?" he asked, turning to Emily. She now stood in the moonlit doorway. Her face bright in the silver light, her thin nose, her marvelous lips, her narrow waist pulled tight by the silk blue dress, her long black hair cascading over her shoulders. She was more beautiful than ever.

"No it isn't." She faced him, her cheeks flushing with anger.

"Why … why is he giving this to me? I don't understand." He thrust his hand out toward her.

"No you don't, do you?" With a huff she spun, gathered her dress, and fled. Henry stood at the door of the carriage, holding her hand he helped her in and latched the door.

"Emily Cotton!" Jefferson shouted from the door of his cabin.

She raised the leather flap on the window.

"I don't need charity."

"Mr. Jefferson Turner, do you know who owns that claim just south of yours down to the gorge?"

"No … no I don't. But what does that have to do with …"

"That's my father's land," her tone was sharp. "That nugget in your hand lay across your boundary, in the open, not ten feet from your claim for the last two years and you never touched it. If you even knew what it was—"

"I knew exactly what it was, Miss Cotton."

"Well good for you, Mr. Turner. Furthermore, Mr. Cotton told me to tell you that since you were kind enough to watch over it for him you might as well have it. And if you were to take it to the assay office you just might find that it will be enough to purchase that claim south of you that he's been wanting to sell for the last year. But then one wonders if you even know where the assay office is since you hardly ever visit it." She threw down the window cover and ordered Henry to take her home.

Turner watched as Henry maneuvered the coach back up the road, urging the pair of bay horses on into the night. It disappeared down the dusty road under the waning moonlight. Jefferson Turner breathed deeply, clenched his fist around the gold nugget, and stood resolutely gazing up at the sparkling glare of the sky.

Christmas indeed.

He let the bitterness drain out of himself for the first time in a while and ruefully realized he would have some apologizing to do soon, both to Emily and to her father. And maybe even to God as well. Then his thoughts drifted just enough to allow a smile to play on his lips.

Jefferson turned the nugget over in his hands and wondered what time tomorrow the Cottons planned on playing charades.

JACK CAVANAUGH

SWEET CHRISTMAS

CHIME.

The shop door swung open. Amy looked up to see an expectant face.

"It came?" Bonnie asked. Christmas music from shopping center speakers crowded in behind her.

Amy held up a single piece of gourmet chocolate in the flat of her hand. The candy was nestled in a gold foil cup.

"I knew I shouldn't have gone to lunch today," Bonnie cried. "I had a feeling."

Amy didn't share her friend's excitement. She slumped in a Louis XV walnut armchair next to a George III mahogany tea table. The Queen's Attic arched over her head on the shop window like an alphabet rainbow. Discarded on the tea table were a one-inch square box, wrapping paper, and ribbon.

"Well? Did you see who delivered it?" Bonnie asked, hanging up her coat and hat.

"I was in the back, packing Mrs. Collingsworth's vase."

"The door sensor …" Bonnie said.

"… didn't go off," Amy finished.

"Zounds!" Bonnie said, shaking her head. "Mystified again … for the third year in a row."

"I know."

"Was there a—?"

Lifting her other hand, Amy held up a slip of paper.

"Did you read it? Of course you read it. You did read it, didn't you?"

Amy gave her a you've-got-to-be-kidding look.

"Well?" Bonnie pressed. "Is it as good as last year?"

"Better."

Pressing her hands to her chest, Bonnie feigned a swoon. "Unbelievable. May I?"

She sighed as she read the slip of paper.

"It is better than last year," she exclaimed. "How come living men can't write poetry this well?" She handed the poem back to Amy and added, "You know, I have a theory about that. Maybe King David is giving him pointers."

Amy shot her a skeptical glance.

"It could happen! I mean, they're both in heaven and David wrote all those psalms in the Bible, didn't he? And they have all the time in the world up there."

Amy stood. "How does Richard do it?" she asked no one in particular. She set the chocolate on the tea table and stared at it. "How? He's been dead three years and still he finds a way to send me a gift every Christmas. Most living husbands don't have that kind of track record."

"I think it's sweet."

"It's unnatural. Dead men don't give their wives Christmas presents."

Bonnie stood over the chocolate. "Is there anything different about it this year? Some kind of clue or something?"

"It's the same as last year, and the year before that," Amy said. "Plain box. Red wrapping paper. White ribbon. A vanilla caramel chocolate with an iced star drawn on top. The same. Always the same."

"What about the paper cup? It's gold foil. All the chocolates I've eaten have had brown paper cups."

Amy examined it. "Same as always. Gold. No markings. I have no idea where it comes from."

"All right … what about the poem? Any clues there?"

Amy studied the slip of paper. "Black ink. Looks like the same paper. White. Good quality."

"And the handwriting?"

"Richard's."

"Are you sure?"

Amy pointed. "The loop on the g, the way he doubles back to cross the *t*. That's Richard's *g* and *t*."

A moment of silence passed between them as they both read it again.

"Richard could have made a living writing cards for Hallmark," Bonnie said.

Amy sighed. "That's what I told him. He said he only had two lines of poetry in him a year."

"Ahhh, how sweet … you were his inspiration."

The door chimed again.

"Mrs. Collingsworth," Amy called. Then, whispering to Bonnie, "Her vase isn't ready."

Bonnie nodded and hurried to the back room.

Mrs. Collingsworth walked in as though the shop was a staging area for her own living room, which it practically was. Thin, with a royal bearing, Amy found her to be a pleasant woman but hard to please.

"Your vase is in the back, Mrs. Collingsworth. I'll go get it."

"Thank you, dear."

Amy hurried to the back room, hoping Bonnie was performing miracles with the vase. At the doorway, she glanced over her shoulder to see Mrs. Collingsworth lower herself into the Louis XV armchair. The woman reached for the chocolate.

"May I?" she said. "I adore Laurents' chocolates."

"No!" Amy cried.

Mrs. Collingsworth pulled her hand back as though the chocolate were a serpent.

Amy lunged to rescue the vanilla caramel, the poem, the wrapping.

"I'm sorry I yelled, Mrs. Collingsworth. It's just that this particular piece of chocolate is a gift with very sentimental— Laurents' chocolates? You know where this piece of chocolate came from?"

"The gold foil cup," said Mrs. Collingsworth. "Laurents' is the only chocolate shop I know that uses them."

"A local shop?"

"La Jolla."

"Bless you, Mrs. Collingsworth. Bless you." Amy threw her arms around the woman and hugged her. "That's the best Christmas present anyone has ever given me."

Mrs. Collingsworth was nonplussed. "You're welcome, dear," she said. "They do make exceptional chocolates."

Amy burst into the back room, past Bonnie who was stuffing handfuls of crinkled paper packing strips into a box.

"Almost done," she said.

Amy didn't hear her. She went straight to the desk and pulled out a phone book.

"What are you—"

"Here!" Amy exulted. "Laurents' Gourmet Chocolates, 1924 Prospect Street, La Jolla."

"A clue?"

"A Christmas present from Mrs. Collingsworth."

ᔕ

"Well, Richard … we've been doing this for seven years now, haven't we?"

Amy sat cross-legged on the living room floor of her apartment. It was midmorning. With no reason to get up early on Christmas, she'd slept in. She sat in front of the blinking lights of her tree. Arrayed in front of her were a picture of Richard, seven poems for seven Christmases, and this year's chocolate.

She picked up the poem from the first year.

> As long as there is Christmas,
> there is hope;
> As long as there is chocolate,
> there is joy.

"Not exactly Shakespeare, but then, you're the only man who I inspired to write poetry. Gotta give you points for that."

She took a bite of the chocolate and picked up the poem from year two. One by one, she worked her way through the poems. Chewing. Reading. Weeping.

∽

A chill of expectation raised bumps on Amy's arms as she surveyed the interior of Laurents' Gourmet Chocolates of La Jolla. The place was spotless white and black with a single showcase stretching the length of shop. Shelved behind a glass display were silver trays with mounds of chocolates. The air was saturated with their odor. Amy concluded this was what heaven must smell like.

Behind the counter was a short, horseshoe-bald man in his early fifties. He wore a smudged white apron and moved with the determination of one whose livelihood depended on filling chocolate orders.

"May I 'elp you?"

The man spoke with a heavy French accent.

"Actually, I didn't come to buy any— Oooo! Those look good!"

The man smiled. "Eet eez a buttery caramel wrapped in Ivory Coast *chocolat au lait,* crowned wees a roasted, salty, caramelized peanut. Would mademoiselle like to try one?"

Amy beamed.

The man handed her a chocolate. Amy took a bite and nearly swooned.

"Exquisite, *non*?" said the man.

"Exquisite, yes," Amy replied. "You can wrap six of them up for me ... no, make that a dozen. I have a friend."

The man smiled. "But of course, mademoiselle."

Amy watched with child's eyes as he reached for a stylized Laurents' Gourmet Chocolate box and began loading it with twelve gold foil paper cups.

"Yes ... those," she cried eagerly. "Those cups."

"Zey come wees zee chocolats," the man said.

Thrusting a hand into her purse, Amy produced a flattened gold foil cup and slapped it on the counter. The man stared at it, not understanding.

"This is one of yours, right?" Amy said.

"Mais, oui. I 'ave boxes and boxes of zem in my back room."

"I'm just interested in this one. Do you recognize it?"

The man looked at her as though she was crazy.

"Maybe this will help," she said. From her purse she pulled the box, wrapping paper, and ribbon and placed them on the counter.

From the man's expression, it didn't help.

"For seven years I've received a single piece of chocolate in a gold cup like this one, wrapped in a box like this one, tied with a ribbon like this one. My husband used to give them to me. Then he died. But I'm still getting them and I want to know who has been sending them to me."

"I give ze single *chocolats* as samples. I do not sell zem."

"It has an icing star on top."

"No stars."

"That's your gold foil, isn't it?"

"May I see zis chocolate?"

Amy cringed. "I ate it. But it had a star on top, like … like …"

She began scanning the showcase, looking for her chocolate. She wasn't having any luck.

"It's a vanilla caramel … square … covered in chocolate … vanilla flavored.… You know?"

"My vanilla caramels. Zey are here."

He pointed to a pyramid of square chocolates with white icing swirls on top.

"Mine has a star," Amy said.

"No stars."

"You must be mistaken. Seven years. Seven chocolates. All with stars on them."

The man shrugged. He couldn't help her.

"And in a box like this," Amy pressed. "You deliver, don't you?"

"We deliver." He examined the box. "Zis is not mine."

"Maybe it's a special order. Could you check your files? My name is Amy Goodman. I live on Garnet—"

"Mademoiselle—"

"… in Pacific Beach."

"Mademoiselle …"

A frantic feeling began welling up inside her. She was so certain she'd learn the truth today and now it was slipping through her fingers.

"Please check your records," she urged again.

"Zer is no need. I can tell you—"

"I wish to speak to the manager. I insist on speaking to the manager!"

Amy felt a presence behind her. A woman customer leaned toward her.

"Mr. Laurents owns the store," the woman whispered.

A new problem confronted Amy. Tears. She fought them back. "Why won't you tell me?" she demanded. "Don't you realize what this is doing to me?"

"Mademoiselle—"

"No! I'm going to stand right here until you tell me who is sending me chocolates every Christmas." To the woman behind her: "I'm sorry, ma'am, but nobody's buying anything until I get some answers."

❧

"But my butter caramels!" Amy whined as the officer led her to her car.

Sgt. Jimmy Burnett of the San Diego Police Department waited while Amy unlocked her car door.

"Sorry, ma'am," he said. "You gave up the right to your chocolates when you chucked them at Mr. Laurents. He could have pressed charges."

"You would have talked him out of it."

"What makes you say that?"

"Think about it. You'd look pretty silly telling a jury the assault weapon was a buttery caramel."

"I suggest you go home and forget all about your mystery chocolates," Sgt. Burnett said.

"You don't know what you're asking," Amy replied. She climbed into her car.

Sgt. Burnett bent down. "I'm not going to have any more trouble with you, am I?"

Amy sighed. The fight had gone out of her. "All I want is to find out how my dead husband manages to send me chocolates every Christmas."

"Go home, ma'am."

Amy slumped behind the wheel, brooding. This couldn't be happening. For the last three days she'd fed on the anticipation that today would be the day she would finally have some answers.

Carefree holiday shoppers strolled sunny Prospect Street, their arms loaded with after-Christmas returns.

Amy inserted her car key into the ignition switch. An economy car zoomed past her and down an alley. A skinny youth with a clipboard jumped out of the car and disappeared into the back door of a shop. Laurents' Gourmet Chocolates was printed on the door.

The delivery boy!

New hope surged in Amy's heart. If she could talk to the delivery boy ... but not here. She couldn't risk Mr. Laurents seeing her.

Twenty minutes later the delivery boy returned to his car, arms loaded with boxes of chocolates and his clipboard. With a puff of exhaust, he was heading down the alley with Amy close behind him.

The first delivery was on Frescota Street, a curving row of million-dollar homes overlooking the Pacific Ocean. The boy jumped out of his car and bounded up a brick entryway. Amy looked for a place to park.

Just as she found one, the delivery boy was back in his car speeding down the street.

"Mr. Laurents must pay him by the delivery!" Amy muttered, racing to catch up with him.

The second delivery was on La Jolla Farms Road. This time Amy was ready. When the delivery boy loped back to his car, counting change in his hand, she punched the accelerator and pulled up next him.

Jumping out of the car, she called, "Can I talk to you for a minute?"

The boy's head snapped up. His eyes grew wide. They darted side to side. When Amy rounded the front of the car, the boy ran around the back, scrambled into his car and was off again, tires squealing.

"Wait! I just want to talk."

Amy bolted for her car and took pursuit. Holiday traffic was on her side. At a signal light on Torrey Pines Road she caught up with him.

She flashed her lights and honked her horn. "Can you pull over? I have a question for you, " she called out her open window.

The boy hit the locks on his doors. At the change of the light, he took off like a jackrabbit.

"Oh, no, you don't," Amy shouted. "You're not getting away from me."

Up and down the streets of La Jolla he tried to shake her. Couldn't. Then, he made a mistake. With Amy on his tail he pulled into the La Jolla Shores parking lot.

"Gotcha!" Amy cried.

She cornered him, pulling up close to his bumper so he couldn't get away. Throwing her car into park, she jumped out. She expected him to run. He didn't.

Through the driver side window Amy saw a boy about eighteen or nineteen years old cowering on the far side of the seat, yelling into a cell phone.

"Hurry. She's trying to get me!"

"Roll down your window," Amy pleaded. "I just want to ask you something." She held up the flattened gold foil cup. "My dead husband paid you to deliver this to me."

The boy shouted louder.

Suddenly, two police cruisers pulled up, rocking crazily as they screeched to a halt. Doors flew open. Officers with guns appeared.

"Not you again," cried Sgt. Burnett. "Lady, it's been less than an hour."

"What? You could have been arrested."

Bonnie stirred her tea. She liked hers strong and with milk. The two women sat at the kitchenette table in Amy's apartment.

Amy fiddled with the gold foil cup. "I don't care," she said. "Really. I can't take it anymore."

"You care," Bonnie said.

"Do you know what I'm going to do next Christmas? Throw the present away unopened."

"You can't do that with chocolate. It's sacrilege."

"I don't care," Amy insisted. "Do you know what these packages are to me? A three-year kernel of corn stuck between my teeth. And now they almost got me arrested."

"Well that delivery boy was wrong," Bonnie said, "you don't look like a crazed psycho to me. And Sgt. Dudley Do-right should have at least allowed you a peek at the delivery records. What harm would it have done?"

Amy sat up suddenly with a thought.

Alerted by the sudden movement, Bonnie set down her teacup. "Uh-oh," she said. "This can't be good."

❧

The bell to the chocolate shop jingled. From behind the counter Laurents looked up. He smiled and said he'd be right with her.

Amy acknowledged his greeting with a nod.

Good. He didn't recognize her.

She pulled the heavy winter coat tight around her neck, adjusted the dark sunglasses and the red scarf over her hair. Milling casually behind the four customers who had preceded her into the shop, she sidled her way to the doorway leading to a back room.

No one seemed to be paying any attention to her. When Mr. Laurents turned away she slipped into the back room.

A quick glace around the room revealed she was alone. Good.

Pulling off scarf and sunglasses she made a quick inventory of the room. It was a typical small business back room with boxes stacked in the corners, a bulletin board plastered with sun-faded notices, and desk stacked high with papers and invoices. She found what she was looking for beside the desk. A grey metal file cabinet. Pulling open the top drawer she fingered through tabs of hanging files.

"Yes," she whispered when she found a file labeled Deliveries.

She shoved with one hand and pulled with the other, then stuck her head into the maw much as a lion tamer does to a lion's mouth.

"What are you doing?"

The voice gave her a start, especially considering it wasn't Mr. Laurents' voice.

Whirling around, Amy came face-to-face with a striking man in his early thirties with wavy brown hair and chiseled cheekbones.

"I asked you what you were doing."

"Um …" Amy stuttered. "Looking for the rest room?"

Her answer seemed to startle the man. His mouth opened slowly into a definite gape.

"Look, I've obviously made a mistake," Amy said, slowly closing the file cabinet drawer. "I'll just be …" As she spoke she wiped her fingerprints from the front of the file cabinet with the cuff of her coat. "… um, going …"

She edged toward the doorway.

He made no attempt to stop her.

But her escape was cut short. Turning, she ran headlong into Laurents. A silver tray with a half dozen chocolates clanged to the floor. Chocolates rolled across the tiles.

"You!" he shouted.

"Mr. Laurents, I can explain."

He grabbed her by the shoulders and shouted, "Call zee police!"

"No!"

Two voices spoke as one. And then, again.

"I can explain."

Amy and the young man exchanged glances. To Laurents he said, "That won't be necessary."

Puzzled, Amy stared at her surprise advocate. And then,

all of a sudden, she knew him. "Noel, is that you?" she asked in disbelief.

"Noel, do you know zees woman?" Laurents asked.

Again, two voices spoke as one.

"Yes."

The young man looked at Laurents, then at Amy.

"We met several years ago," Noel said.

"What are you doing here?" Amy asked.

The young man clutched a batch of papers in his hand. Slowly, he walked to the desk and set them down.

"I'll take care of this, Pop," he said.

Laurents was reluctant to release Amy. When he did, he said, "I'll be in zee front."

Before leaving them, Laurents picked up the tray and the chocolates. Amy supposed he didn't want to leave any ammunition within reach.

No sooner had he left than Amy took up her case. "Laurents is your father? Don't tell me you're the one who's been delivering the chocolates to me every year."

Noel didn't look at her. "Yes," he said.

His confession prompted a rush of emotion. Now that she was close to learning the truth, she was afraid to hear it. But she had to know. She had to.

"Who's behind this?" she cried. "Do you realize what a nightmare this has been for me?"

He hung his head and said nothing.

"At first it was cool," Amy said. "Romantic, you know? Even the fourth one, the year Richard died. It made me feel hopeful, you know what I mean? It made me believe. After all, it was Christmas. A time of hope. A time of miracles. And I really made myself believe that the doctor was going to call …"

A surge of emotions choked her.

"… and that he would say … it was a mistake … just a stupid mistake … a mix-up at the lab, and Richard really wasn't … really wasn't …"

Amy fumbled in her pocket until she found a tissue.

"But then … oh God help me, it was three years ago today … I knew there would be no miracle. And I thought, well … that's it, you know? It's over. He's gone. But it wasn't over, was it? Because the next Christmas I get this little present with a single piece of chocolate in it … from Richard! I get a Christmas present from my dead husband! Now what is a woman supposed to do when that happens? I mean, really … what?"

Noel fidgeted uneasily. "I … we … I guess we never thought …"

Fighting back tears, Amy sniffed angrily and crossed her arms.

"Well, I hope you got paid well, that's all I can say. But then, you're probably one of those guys who do it just for kicks. You get your jollies watching people being made to look like fools."

"No, it wasn't like that at all."

"Then tell me, what was it like?"

Noel reached beside the desk for a briefcase. He opened it. Inside was red wrapping paper and white ribbon. There was also a yellow pad with line after line of practice sentences, the kind a person would write to imitate someone's handwriting.

"You?" Amy cried. "You didn't just deliver the package. It's been you all along, hasn't it? You're some kind of copy-cat, copy-cat—"

"Gift giver?" Noel said.

From the briefcase he pulled a manila folder and from the folder a piece of paper, which he handed to her. "The original invoice," he said.

In big block letters was written: special order: star = hope.

It was dated seven years ago.

"I met your husband at UCSD. We took a class together. Introduction to Poetry."

Amy shook her head. "Richard was studying to write screenplays. He never took a poetry class."

"Tuesdays and Thursdays. Seven to ten at night."

"I'm telling you, Richard never took a poetry class."

"How about a short-story class?"

Amy thought. "Yes, he took a class on short stories. Tuesday and Thursday…"

Noel laughed. "None of us told our friends we were taking a poetry class. Short stories sounded more manly."

Noel pulled an envelope from the manila folder.

"He told me to give you this if ever you caught me delivering the chocolate."

Amy stared at the envelope. With trembling hand, she took it.

It was sealed and it had her name printed on the outside in Richard's handwriting. Noel handed her a letter opener. Her hand shook as she ripped open the envelope.

> *My darling Amy,*
> *You remember Noel Laurents. If you're reading this letter, it means something went awry and you suspect him of some very questionable activity …*

The letter went on to describe how the two men met at school in a short-story class and become friends, how Richard asked Noel to watch out for her following his death.

> *My dearest, remember when I told you that great events swing on …*

"What was Richard thinking?" Amy cried, dropping her hand. "What were you thinking?"

Noel winced.

"I'm calling the police!"

"The police?"

"Or the FBI. Or Homeland Security. Somebody! There's gotta be a law somewhere on the books that—"

"Prevents a man from writing love poetry to a woman?"

Amy took a step back. "You don't even know me."

"Not true. Richard told me all about you. He loved you so much. When he knew his time was close, he asked me to watch over of you. At first I wasn't going to try the poetry. But I was there when Richard's last chocolate was delivered. At the Queen's Attic. We watched you through the window, and I saw the expression on your face when you read the poem."

A side of Amy wanted to give the guy a break. Another side of her wanted to break his neck.

"Why didn't you just tell me?"

Noel looked down. "I couldn't."

"Why? Are you married? I've heard about you French men."

Laughing, he said, "I saw the way you and Richard were together. You were always waiting for him after class. I saw the way you looked at him. A voice inside told me you could never love another man as deeply as you loved Richard. I knew I couldn't compete with a fairytale romance."

"I can tell you this much," Amy said. "You certainly can't do it by hiding behind a dead man. And you can't do it by pining from a distance."

She turned to leave, then turned back.

"Just because I'm leaving doesn't mean I'm still not angry at you. This whole thing is just … just …"

She turned to leave, then turned back.

"And one more thing … Last year's poem was good. I mean, really, really good."

Noel grinned. "One of my better moments."

"You're a good writer."

He shook his head. "Nah, I only seem to have two good lines in me a year."

It was Amy's turn to smile. She turned to leave, then turned back.

"And let's get one thing straight. These Christmas chocolates and poems end right now, got it? Three years of torture is enough."

She turned to leave, then turned back again.

"But that doesn't mean you can't deliver chocolates other times of the year. Say, January. Maybe the seventh. Which happens to be—"

"Your birthday."

Amy shot him a glance. "I don't even want to know how you know that."

She turned to leave, then turned back.

"And if you want to stop by and, you know, just go for a walk or get some coffee or something, that would be fine too."

She turned to leave, then turned back.

"Only give me a week … no, five … no, three days. It's going to take at least that long to cry this out."

ஐ

Amy sat on the floor of her apartment in front of the Christmas tree with a box of tissues at her side and wadded tissues looking like snowballs scattered about her.

> *My dearest, remember when I told you that great events swing on small hinges? Well, I'm hoping romance will swing on a piece of chocolate.*
>
> *Don't be angry with me. I know how you hated it whenever I attempted to point out possible suitors for you after I was gone. But just because I'm dead doesn't mean I've stopped wanting to make you happy. I think Noel can make you happy.*
>
> *Darling, give love a chance. I'm hoping that a piece of chocolate and the Christmas season will find a way to introduce you to Noel. I give it two years. You should know by then whether or not you like each other.*
>
> *As for me? You will always be my one and only.*
>
> *Yours forever,*
> *Richard*

Amy toyed with the gold foil cup. "Could be worse," she said aloud. "Noel is, after all, the heir to a chocolate shop."

TERRY BURNS

AN E-MAIL FOR CHRISTMAS

CORPORAL MIKE COTTON SAT on his cot holding the combat boot he had just removed, seeming to lack the will to drop it. His shoulders slumped and he stared at the floor, anguish on his face.

"This is the worst day since we've been over here."

Sergeant Steve Smith, the squad leader, nodded. He knew

the look. "It doesn't seem much like Christmas when we look out and see sand and Humvees instead of snow and sleighs."

Both men wore desert camouflage, the uniform of the day in the field in Iraq. Beyond that they had little in common. Mike was a big man with a baby face framed and accented by dark-brown hair and eyebrows. Steve looked older than his twenty-six years, with unruly blond hair and an ever-present grin that made his orders easier to take. His men would charge hell with a bucket of water for him.

Mike finally tossed his first boot and began to unlace the other one. "No, it's not that. We got a good meal, and they worked really hard making it all feel festive. If it were just me, I'd be okay with that. It's my family, my kids, knowing what it's doing to their Christmas, me not being there with them."

The perpetual smile faded from Steve's face. "I see. Well, eight-hour time difference, it's midafternoon back in Texas. I bet she's already fired off an e-mail telling you all about it. So what are you doing in here? Let's head over to the com tent." Steve rose from his cot and stepped over to stand by the door.

"That's not a bad idea." Mike quickly relaced his boot and reached to retrieve the other.

In the com tent they found coffee and waited impatiently for time on one of the computers. It seemed to take forever. When Mike finally got on a machine he immediately logged onto his e-mail. A message from his wife, Elisabeth, waited in bold type. He clicked on it eagerly, not knowing whether he would find encouragement or something that would further depress him. Even if she felt down, she would try to keep it upbeat and cheerful; he knew that. But he could always tell when his distance from home was weighing on her heart.

> *Dear Mike,*
>> *Some times are harder for you to be away from us than others.*

There was no hiding her emotion this time. A lump came into his throat and a heaviness descended on his chest.

> *The kids and I have been decorating for Christmas and trying hard to get into the holiday spirit, but it has been very difficult.*

"You get one from home?" Steve put his hand on his friend's shoulder.

Mike glanced over his shoulder, "Yes, but I'm beginning to wish I hadn't."

"Sorry, man, I'll leave you alone."

Mike kept his friend from turning away with a hand on his forearm. "You didn't have anything?"

"No, I've got a few people who send me stuff from time to time, but the army is my family. I've got nobody back at home."

"Pull up a chair then. Good or bad, you can share it with me."

Steve positioned a chair so he could see the monitor from it. Mike scrolled down to reveal more text, and began to read:

> *We were feeling pretty sorry for ourselves*
> *Christmas Eve, I'll admit it.*

"Aw man," Steve said, "I see what you mean."

"I can just see her, I know the look; I've even caused it on occasion by doing something stupid. She doesn't have to say a word; I start trying to make it right as soon as I see the pain in her face. I want to run home right now and erase that look, you know what I mean?"

"Hey, you're talking to a confirmed bachelor here, but I envy you having that strong a connection with her, I really do. Go on; go on, what's she saying?"

Together the two soldiers leaned over to follow the words as Mike read them aloud.

> *Then Clare (she's our small-group leader now)*
> *called and asked if she and some others could*
> *pick us up for the candlelight Christmas Eve*
> *service. I thought that might help, so I agreed. I*
> *suppose she called from her cell phone, because it*
> *took no time at all for her to be here.*

Mike's voice got a little husky. He cleared his throat and continued:

*What a surprise we got when we got to the
church. It was beautiful, lit by nothing but
candles in the windows, green garlands on the
ends of all the pews. Then it stopped me in my
tracks when I got to the pew where we usually sit.*

*Your place was marked by a draped American
flag.*

*Not folded—that might have brought the
wrong image to mind—but draped on the back of
the seat with your picture sitting on it. I started
to cry and they all gathered around me. Their
touch was so comforting.*

Steve called out to some soldiers drinking coffee nearby.
"You guys need to see this." He looked at his friend. "That all
right, Mike?"

"Sure, why not?"

Several men and women walked over to stand behind
them. Mike's voice had betrayed him on the last passage so
Steve began to read the e-mail aloud, catching them up on the
previous part, then picking up from there:

*Brother Bill preached a sermon on sacrifice.
He said we should all be mindful of the sacrifices
our loved ones are making being away from their
families, protecting our freedom and the freedom
of the Iraqi people. I thought my heart would*

stop when he reminded us quietly that some had
paid an even higher cost.

Someone murmured from behind Mike. "You got a special lady there."

"You think other churches might be doing this?" another wondered aloud.

Mike smiled at them, "It wouldn't surprise me for this to be going on all over the country."

"You guys let the man read," a voice in the back ordered. The group had already nearly doubled in size.

Steve scooted his chair a little closer.

He went on in his sermon to talk about the
sacrifice that Jesus made for us, going to the cross
to redeem us from our sins.

Mike nodded, "Yeah, we get to feeling like we're really putting it on the line, but that puts it into perspective."

A young soldier looked terribly serious, "I saw that movie. You know the one, where they treated that dude so bad then nailed him up on that cross? I don't really understand what it's all about, but I can't get it out of my head. They really put him through it, and he just took it, man, he just took it."

"We need to talk, Samuel," Mike smiled, "right after I finish, okay?"

The soldier nodded. They held eye contact for several

moments and Mike could tell the young man had reached a point where he did need to talk to somebody about it.

Steve resumed his reading.

> *Brother Bill said tomorrow we'd be celebrating the birth of Jesus, not his death. He wrapped up his talk and then everybody gathered around us.*
>
> *Mike, you know it's a small church, and you're the only one we have serving right now. It's as if the whole church is your family, and they're all praying for you and for those you're serving with.*

Steve turned toward his friend, an incredulous look on his face. "I never knew anybody ever prayed for me."

Mike put a hand on his shoulder. "All the time, Steve, all the time."

The feisty little sergeant couldn't seem to find any words. "I don't know what to say. I never knew."

"That's my fault. I should have told you."

"Don't that beat all?" He turned his attention back to the message.

> *By the time we got home a group of carolers was there. They all carried candles and were singing so beautifully. In only minutes it seemed like everyone in the neighborhood had joined them, and it was just wonderful.*

> *You remember that crotchety old man over on
> the corner, Mr. Sandoval? He invited everyone
> over to his house for refreshments. He made up
> some spiced apple cider, and we had a fine time.*

"I'd like a little of that myself," somebody said.

"I can take care of that," the mess sergeant said, "but not right now, OK? I want to hear the rest of this too."

"Spiced cider does sound good," Steve said. "Looks like she's talking about the next day now. She says:

> *Christmas morning we got up at the break of
> dawn, you know how the kids run in to see what
> Santa left. I guess they're all like that.*

Steve looked at those behind him. "We sure were when I was little.'"

A murmur of assent came from behind them, "My kids don't wait till dawn. They start begging to open presents at midnight!"

"Ain't it the truth?"

In the field soldiers habitually wore what they called their "game faces," insulating themselves from many of the problems they faced by drawing inside, not showing their feelings to those around them. There were no game faces in the room now. These were softer faces, full. People allowing themselves to feel.

Steve read on.

*I was afraid they might be disappointed.
Money is still pretty tight. I couldn't get
everything, as you know, but I tried to get them
each at least one thing they really wanted.*

*Before we could open any gifts there was a
knock on the door. I opened it and there were
several Marines standing there in dress blues,
and one wearing a red suit with a white beard.
You could hardly see them for all the presents
they were carrying.*

The mess sergeant laughed. "Them Gyrenes are all right.
They do that every year."

Mike nodded. "I'll say they're all right. I'm sure they have
to be taking time away from their own families to come look
after mine. I've seen that Toys for Tots thing on TV most of my
life and it never really hit home to me until now."

Steve smiled, "You gonna yammer or are we going to finish reading this?"

"Sorry, go ahead."

"Looks like they had a big time with those marines, and
they even stayed to play with them and put things together."

"Some assembly required," a guy muttered. "Why don't
they just say 'you're going to be up all night with this.'"

Steve read on: "But she says that right after the marines
left, she got a call from the commanding officer at the Army

Reserve Center. There's still a contingent there, you know?"

"Lucky stiffs," somebody said. "Done their time or didn't have to come for some reason."

Steve shook his head, "That bunch is all right too; listen to this:

> *He sent a Humvee for us. The kids really got a kick out of that. They had asked all the dependents with relatives away from home down to have a Christmas meal with the unit.*
>
> *When we arrived they formed the company for inspection. They did a roll call, and when they came to your name somebody in the back said, "Deployed, Sir! Standing tall in Iraq." Someone answered for every soldier that wasn't there. They think about you guys over there a lot.*
>
> *They had a field kitchen set up and said it would give us an idea of what you were eating. Actually, he said you would probably even be eating a little better than what they were set up to do, but it'd give us an idea of the experience. I thought the food was good, and we were treated royally.*
>
> *Of course as soon as I got home I put the kids down for a nap and rushed in here to tell you all about it. I know it's late over there and you*

probably won't read this until tomorrow. I just
want to tell you how much I love you and …

Steve cleared his throat. "Well it starts getting a little personal here so I'll let you read the rest of it yourself." He got up, "Besides, didn't I hear something about some spiced cider?"

The soldiers started filing out heading for the mess tent, talking quietly among themselves. Fifteen minutes later Mike came in. "I answered her e-mail."

"Figured you would. You seem to be in better spirits."

"I think they had a good Christmas, thanks to all the people back home that care about them, and a bunch of guys that go above and beyond the call of duty. If they had a good Christmas, then I had a good Christmas."

"Thanks for sharing, Mike. I think you gave us all a good Christmas."

"Thank you for making me do it. I would have just gone to bed and laid awake stewing in my own juices. For somebody who doesn't have family, you sure knew what I needed."

"I feel like I picked up a little family myself tonight."

Across the tent someone started singing "Silent Night" and everyone joined in. They sang every carol they knew, the sound drawing people back out of their rack from all over the camp.

During the singing, Mike went over to put his arm around his friend's shoulder. "Samuel, how about you and I go over here and talk about that movie you saw?"

ROBIN JONES GUNN

CHRISTMAS GRACE

GRACE ENTERED THE DARKNESS one night in Bethlehem when God wrapped himself in flesh and was laid in a manger. For over two thousand years evidence of this Grace—this Light of the World—has continued to shine in the darkness. I know this Grace. I've seen this Light many times. Two distinct times came on Christmas, and with the Light came hope. The first time I was only ten years old …

ဆာ

"It's time you kids learned the true meaning of Christmas," my dad announced one night at the dinner table. From the way my mom was grinning, I knew we were doomed.

"Our family has become too materialistic. This year

we're going to change all that. Instead of buying presents, we're going on a trip."

"To Bethlehem?" my brother asked. (He was eight. You know how third graders can be.)

"No. To Oregon," Dad said.

"Oregon?" we echoed.

My mom kept grinning. "We're going to Corvallis to spend the holidays with the Anderson family." The Andersons were family friends who had moved out of state.

"But mom!" my brother moaned. "When the Andersons lived here they never celebrated Christmas! No trees, no lights, no presents!"

"And no fun," I added with a groan.

"We'll still have lots of fun," she said. "We may even have snow!" For a person who'd moved to Southern California years ago to escape the Midwest winters, I wondered why all the sudden excitement over snow.

My sister was the only one not complaining. She just sat there with this dreamy look on her face. And I knew why. The Andersons' oldest boy, Steve, was her age—a big, mature, seventh grader. I was only in sixth grade, but I knew the look of puppy love when I saw it.

My dad seemed awfully excited about our "back to nature" trip to Oregon. As we three long-legged kids squished into the back seat of our old Ford station wagon, he let us know that we were driving straight through. We would stop only for gas, he explained. No extra bathroom stops or soda pop stops. No emergency stops. He did stop once, though—when my brother threw up in his shoe. You see, he had to throw up and he knew Dad wouldn't stop, so he took off his shoe and … it was gross.

When we got to the Andersons', it was pouring rain. No snow. We huddled on their doorstep like refugees fleeing from a wayward middle-class America, searching for the true meaning of home, family, and Christmas.

"Oh, you poor dears!" Mrs. Anderson exclaimed. "Come right in. I've been keeping dinner warm for you."

We slumped around the large dining room table as she pulled from the oven a pan of eggplants stuffed with ground turkey, with shriveled little pimentos on top. "And if you're really hungry," she said, "I've got a fresh batch of tofu." My brother ran to the bathroom and got sick again. I considered doing the same.

The next morning was Christmas Eve day. Mrs. Anderson gave us oatmeal for breakfast. My brother was the only one who ate all of his. My sister just sat there, giggling at everything Steve said. I didn't feel much Christmas spirit developing within me yet. But then my mom came in and said my dad and Mr. Anderson were going to drive the six of us kids to the snow!

We piled into the back of the Andersons' pickup truck

and our mothers layered us with army blankets. My sister sat next to Steve. Really close.

"Have lots of fun!" Mrs. Anderson said. "When you get back, we'll have some surprises for you!" I hoped none of her surprises involved tofu.

It was cold in the back of that truck. We all started fighting over the blankets and finally ended up scrunched down and huddled together like a bunch of baby birds waiting for their big, fat, warm mama bird to come sit on them. Suddenly the truck stopped. We propped our heads up and there, on the side of the road, was snow—real live snow. I was about to experience my first white Christmas!

We fought over who got to use the toboggan first and charged to the top of the hill. My dad kept throwing snowballs at us, laughing all the while at how our feeble retaliations never went more than two feet in the air before self-destructing. Personally, I felt the snow was cold and wet and highly overrated. But the best part of the trip was still ahead—the ride home in the back of the truck.

We huddled together and told jokes all the way. Whenever Steve told a joke my sister laughed loudest. Then we had a burping contest. My brother usually is the best burper, but he said that every time he tried to burp he felt oatmeal mixed with root beer in his throat and we told him he was disqualified.

Steve's burps were the best, but then all of a sudden I let

out a real corker and my sister said, "Ewww! That's disgusting!" But Steve thought it was totally cool. He said he'd never met a girl who could burp like that.

Mrs. Anderson's surprise came in a Woolworth's bag. One for me and one for my sister. She presented them to us that evening with such enthusiasm. "I know we're not exchanging gifts, but I just had to get a little something for you two girls." We pulled from our bags the ugliest turquoise and pink polka-dot rain hats the world has ever seen. I decided then and there that it's better not to get a single thing for Christmas than to get a turquoise and pink polka-dot rain hat. Especially in Oregon, where it rains all the time and you don't have an excuse for not wearing it.

Christmas Day dawned and our materialistically warped family sat in the living room looking at each other. There was no tree to admire, no gifts to unwrap, no baking turkey smells wafting from the kitchen. Then Mr. Anderson bounced in with "good news." He'd arranged for us to borrow their church's bus so that we could all go to the beach. I knew we were dead meat.

It rained the whole way there, and of course that meant my sister and I had to bring our charming rain hats. After endless bumps in the back of the bus we arrived at the beach, only to hear the adults decide it was raining too hard and the wind was too fierce for us even to get out. We'd eat our picnic lunch in the bus and then turn around and go home.

By now I was feeling pretty cold and damp and miserable and couldn't care less if I ever discovered the true meaning of Christmas. Mrs. Anderson passed around the sandwiches. I peeked between two tough pieces of rye bread and looked up at her questioningly.

"Deviled Spam with sweet pickle relish," she said proudly. "The pickles came from our own garden." Somehow, I wasn't surprised.

I turned to my sister and whispered, "Let's make a Sister's Secret Pact. Let's both promise that when we grow up and get married and have children, we'll never make our families go to Oregon for Christmas."

"And," she added quietly, "we'll never make our children eat deviled Spam."

We linked pinkies, closed our eyes, and the promise was sealed.

After devouring three of his wife's deviled Spam sandwiches, Mr. Anderson tried to back the bus onto the pavement. That's when it happened. Clunk! Hiss! Shoosh! Steve was the first to figure it out. "Hey, Dad! I think we got a flat tire."

Mr. Anderson climbed out to have a look. My dad followed him. They both scurried back into the bus, soaking wet.

"It's a flat all right. You kids be careful, now. We'll have to jack this thing up and change the tire with you inside."

We all squealed with delight. Now we'd have some real fun! We pressed our faces against the window as our dads braved the storm, trying to figure out how to secure the jack. Dad ran back into the bus and said, "The wind is blowing the rain in our faces so we can barely see. Do you have a towel we can hold over our heads?"

"Here!" my sister and I said in unison. "You can use these!" We graciously held out our beloved rain hats. My dad took the hats and tugged mine down over his ears. I had never seen anything so funny in all my ten years and I started laughing. Our dads fought and tugged and sloshed around trying to change that tire and we couldn't stop laughing. They made Laurel and Hardy look like amateurs.

Then a gust of wind grabbed my hat off my dad's head and teasingly rolled it through the air toward the ocean. Dad actually started running after it! But it was too late. The hat was gone forever, and I laughed until I cried.

"Don't cry, dear," Mrs. Anderson consoled me. "I'll get you another one." My sister kicked me, and I swallowed the laughter until my throat throbbed.

Just then my dad stepped back in the bus completely drenched, looking like a defeated man. "There's no spare," he shouted over the wind. "This bus has no spare tire." Nobody was laughing anymore.

Four hours later, the moms and kids were still sitting in the bus, shivering, waiting for the dads to return from their long walk to find help. The rain and wind had subsided and it was so dark that we could no longer see the rocks or the shoreline.

Someone started singing. I think it was Mrs. Anderson. "Silent night, holy night, all is calm, all is bright ..." We all joined in like our lives depended on it and continued with "Away in the Manger," "Hark the Herald Angels Sing," and "Joy to the World." When we got to the part about "Let every heart prepare him room, and heaven and nature sing," I was staring out the window into the darkness. Suddenly it was all there—the star, the shepherds, the angels, Mary, Joseph, and a tiny baby in a manger. It was Christmas.

Even in a broken-down bus, on the wild Oregon coast, it was the birthday of a King.

I don't think anybody else saw what I saw, all that light in the darkness. I closed my eyes and imagined that Jesus was sitting next to me on the torn vinyl seat. He seemed so close. So real. I made sure no one was looking, and then I pretended to rest my head against his shoulder. Very softly, I told him how happy I was that he had chosen to spend his birthday with me.

We got home from our adventure after midnight. The adults all laughed about how they'd never do that again and about what a mistake it had been. But when I crawled into my sleeping bag on the floor next to my sister, I felt something different.

I poked her to make sure she wasn't asleep yet. "I might have to make a change in our Sister's Secret Pact," I said solemnly.

"Leave me alone," she grumbled.

"I'm afraid to tell you this, but when I grow up and get married, I might take my kids to Oregon for Christmas."

"Oh," she snorted. "That's OK. Just don't change the part about making them eat deviled Spam."

"Don't worry," I promised. "I never will."

ଛ

Years later, my Christmases had grown to include a husband of my own, two wonderful children, and more family and laughter than I could have hoped for. Yet in the midst of such fullness of life one distinct Christmas was shadowed by the kind of darkness that comes after a sad loss. All of us needed Grace the year we celebrated Christmas without Grandma Kay....

ଛ

"OK," I agreed with my husband. "We'll invite your family here for Christmas. But you know it's going to be hard for everyone since your mom passed away."

"I know," he said. "That's why we all need to be together."

I sort of agreed with him. But I knew I couldn't take Kay's place as hostess. I was still grieving myself and didn't feel I could be responsible for the emotional atmosphere on our first holiday without her.

I made all the preparations—cookies, decorations, presents—then welcomed Ross's family on Christmas Eve with open arms as I braced myself for a holiday punctuated by sorrow. That evening at church, our clan filled the entire back section. Afterwards, at home, the kids scampered upstairs and my husband shouted, "Five minutes!" The adults settled in the living room as he began to read from Luke chapter two.

At verse eight, our six-year-old, Rachel, appeared at the top of the stairs wearing her brother's bathrobe, a shawl over her head, and carrying a stuffed lamb under her arm. She struck a pose and stared at the light fixture over the dining room table as if an angel had just appeared.

My father-in-law chuckled, "Look at her! You'd think she could really hear heavenly voices."

Next came Mary, one of my nieces who'd donned the blue bridesmaid dress I wore in my sister's wedding. I knew then that the kids had gotten into my closet. The plastic baby Jesus fit nicely under the full skirt of the blue dress. My son, appearing as Joseph, discreetly turned his head as Mary "brought forth" her firstborn son on the living room floor, wrapped him in a dish towel, and laid him in the laundry basket.

We heard a commotion as my husband turned to Matthew 2 and read the cue for the Magi. He repeated it, louder, "We saw his star in the east and have come to worship him."

One of my junior high-age nephews whispered "You go first!" and pushed his older brother out of the bedroom into full view. Slowly, the ultimate wise man descended with Rachel's black tutu on his head and bearing a large bottle of canola oil.

The adults burst out laughing and I did too, until I realized what he was wearing. It was a gold brocade dress with pearls and sequins that circled the neck and shimmered down the entire left side. Obviously the kids had gone through the bags I'd brought home after we'd cleaned out Kay's closet. Bags filled with shoes, hats, a few dresses, and some scarves that still smelled like her.

The laughter quickly diminished when my father-in-law said, "Hey! That's Kay's dress! What are you doing wearing her dress?"

Rachel looked at Grandpa from her perch at the top of the staircase. "Grandma doesn't mind if he uses it," she said. "I know she doesn't."

We all glanced silently at each other.

I didn't doubt that Rachel had an inside track into her grandma's heart. Kay had been there the day she was born, waiting all night in the hospital, holding a vase with two pink roses picked from her garden. She'd carried the roses through two airports and on the hour-long flight, telling everyone who she was going to see: "My son, his wife, my grandson, and the granddaughter I've been waiting for."

I'd slept with the two pink roses on my nightstand and my baby girl next to me in her bassinet. When I awoke early in the morning to nurse my squirming, squealing infant, I noticed a red mark on her cheek. Was it blood? A birthmark I hadn't noticed before?

No, it was lipstick. Grandma Kay had visited her first granddaughter sometime during the night.

It was Grandma Kay who taught Rachel the three silent squeezes. A squeeze-squeeze-squeeze of the hand means "I-love-you." My introduction to the squeezes was in the bride's dressing room on my wedding day. Kay slid past the wedding coordinator and photographer. In all the flurry, she quietly slipped her soft hand into mine and squeezed it three times. After that, I felt the silent squeezes many times. We all did.

When we got the call last year that Kay had gone into diabetic coma, Ross caught the next plane home. Our children and I prayed this would only be a close call, like so many others in the past two years. But Kay didn't come out of it this time. A week later, we tried to accept the doctor's diagnosis that it was only a matter of days. The children seemed to understand that all we could do was wait.

One night that week Rachel couldn't sleep. I brought

her to bed with me but she wouldn't settle down. Crying, she said she wanted to talk to her Grandma.

"Just have Daddy put the phone up to her ear," she pleaded. "I know she'll hear me."

It was 10:30 p.m. I called the hospital and asked for Kay's room. My husband answered at her bedside. I watched my daughter sit up straight and take a deep breath.

"OK, Rachel," my husband said. "You'll have to talk loud because there are noisy machines helping Grandma breathe."

"Grandma, it's me, Rachel!" she shouted. "I wanted to tell you good night. I'll see you in heaven."

Rachel handed me the phone and nestled down under the covers. "Oh," she said, springing up, "Tell Daddy to give Grandma three squeezes for me."

Two days later, Grandma Kay died. She had left clear instructions to the family: She wanted to be cremated and her ashes scattered over the Pacific Ocean, whose waves she had gazed at every day from her kitchen window.

Rachel sat with her cousin during the memorial service, and I couldn't help but notice her unusual calm and poise. She told everyone, "Grandma is going to see Noah and the real Rachel and David, but not Goliath, I don't think."

When we boarded the chartered yacht in Newport Beach to carry out Kay's wishes, the cousins all sported pudgy orange life jackets and nibbled chips and M&M's. It was a painfully gorgeous summer evening, and I missed Kay so much. But saying good-bye to her as the sun set and the brisk ocean wind flew against our faces was much sweeter than huddling around a sealed box. In her death, as in life, she thought first of what others would enjoy.

Earlier that afternoon, with a dozen flower baskets sitting all over, Rachel had secretly instructed her cousins to "pick a bouquet for Grandma to take on the boat." As the yacht sped out to sea, the cousins retrieved their flowers and tossed them into the water in turn, saying good-bye to Grandma Kay that sun-kissed Southern California evening.

I bit my lower lip when I saw Rachel's bouquet. It was centered with two pink roses. She tossed it overboard, the last one to say good-bye.

Now, Christmas Eve, in our snow-covered house, Rachel was the first to welcome Grandma's memory into our celebration.

"Really, Grandpa," she continued to plead. "Grandma wouldn't mind."

We all knew Rachel was right. Grandma Kay wouldn't have cared if her grandchildren found delight in anything that belonged to her. If the dress had been embroidered with pure 24-karat gold, Grandma Kay wouldn't have minded a bit.

Grandpa nodded. The pageant continued. The next wise guy paraded down the stairs, stumbling on his too-big bathrobe, a towel wrapped around his head and bearing a jumbo-sized Lawry's Seasoned Salt. He laid it at the laundry basket.

My husband read about the shepherd's returning, "glorifying and praising God for all the things they had heard and seen, just as they had been told."

Then the cast took a bow and scrambled for the kitchen where they fought over lighting the candle on Jesus' birthday cake.

When we started singing "Happy Birthday" to Jesus, I looked down at the little shepherds standing next to me. Maybe Grandpa was right. Maybe she really did hear heavenly voices.

Then Rachel's small, warm hand nuzzled its way into mine. I felt my daughter give me three silent squeezes and once again, Christmas Grace came into the dark places and poured out light. Light that was given to us that first Christmas, wrapped in flesh. Jesus. The gift of Grace that fills us with hope.

JOSEPH HILLEY

EDGAR'S GIFT

KATHLEEN LAY IN BED and listened to the wind howl-
ing around the corner of the house. It roared past the
window and rattled that loose piece of tin on the roof
near the back porch. With each gust a chilling draft
seeped through the cracks in the wall and drifted across
the bed. She pulled the covers up to her chin and lay
there, listening.

The house was made of rough pine lumber and had
unfinished interior walls that echoed with every breath,
every voice, every footstep. She knew when someone
turned over in bed. When a child yawned. Sometimes, she
could hear stomachs growling when they'd had too little to
eat for supper.

In the bed beside her lay Edgar, her husband. They
had married when she was thirteen, and he'd been beside

her every night since. She listened as he snored softly and watched as his chest rose and fell against the pile of quilts and blankets that covered them.

Silver light from a bright winter moon streamed through the thin curtains on the windows and cast a gray glow across the room. Though it was late, she could see every detail as if it were the middle of the day. The dresser along the wall at the end of the bed. The mirror above it. The picture of her parents on the wall across from the window. The chair near the door with Edgar's overalls hanging on the back. In the glow of the moonlight she could see his gold watch chain draped from a pocket on the bib to a buttonhole near the strap on the left side. The watch and chain had been his father's, a gift to Edgar from his mother on her son's wedding day.

Down the hall, a bed creaked. Then … something else. She pushed the quilt away from her neck and cocked her head to one side. A child's whisper drifted through the night.

"… and ain't nobody been to town in … I can't remember when."

The voice was lost in a gust of wind but she knew it was Guy, her youngest. Born the day after Christmas, nine years ago. One last gift to herself.

The wind faded away, whistling through the pines behind the barn. She heard him again.

"I know it's asking a lot, but I'd really like a ball. One of them kind you have to air up. Like they play basketball with. I seen one at school one day. Billy Autwell has one. I ain't asking for his. Just one like it. Amen."

The bed creaked. She heard him roll over and pull the covers over his head.

She wanted to grab the quilt and throw it aside. Slip down the hall. Hold him close. Tell him everything would be all right. Of course he could have a ball for Christmas. Just think of the fun he would have. Not to worry. Everything would work out right.

But there was nothing she could do.

Tears came to her eyes. She'd seen him by the barn shooting a ball at that rim he'd made from a rusted bucket they found at the edge of the field when they were chopping up the cotton stalks. He'd cut the bottom out of it and rigged it above the door, then spent the afternoons shooting at it with a foam ball he'd had since … since the time they were on Mr. Nunnally's place and things had been a little better. That seemed a long time ago.

Now, there he was, lying in the cold down the hall. Praying.

It had been hard going for a while now. Somebody said the stock market had crashed last year and that was making it tough on everyone this year. Stock market. She wasn't sure what a stock market was, or how one crashed, or how it could affect her all the way down there on the little plot of ground they cropped on shares. She only knew cotton prices were so low they didn't have money to buy shoes for their children. And the traveling peddler with his old jalopy of a truck didn't come by as often as before, and when he did he traded her half as much sugar for a dozen eggs as he used to. And the hardpan Alabama clay wasn't as kind or as fruitful or as generous as it had been in the past.

Shadows of the trees swaying in the moonlight danced across the curtains. She glanced up at the window and wiggled her toes to make sure they weren't frozen.

Shoes.

Nobody had new shoes. She could make shirts. Bleach the print out of the flour sacks, use them for cloth. Wash them a few times and they'd get smooth and soft. She knew how to do that. She knew how to cut up a worn-out pair of pants to patch the knees on their overalls. But shoes.... Shoes were different.

And Christmas.

Christmas was just days away. It had been Monday night when they went to bed. She wasn't sure what time it was right then but when the sun came up in a little while it would be Tuesday. Wednesday would be Christmas Eve. A long, slow sigh escaped her. Hard to think about Christmas when you had to patch the soles of your shoes with cardboard every night.

Edgar rolled over in bed and sleepily draped an arm across her shoulder. Tears ran from her eyes and dripped onto the sheet.

Morning came before she was ready. She crawled out of bed, slipped on her dress, and wrapped a blanket over her shoulders. In the kitchen she took a few pieces of kindling from the box by the door and built a fire in the woodstove. There were biscuits to bake. Maybe a little gravy if the cow gave them enough milk. The cow. It would give a little more if they had something to feed it besides corn shucks.

She took the wooden bowl from the cabinet and scooped a cupful of flour from the canister. She poured it in the bowl and began to work it with her fingers.

In a few minutes the back door opened and Edgar came in with the egg basket. He set it on the table and kissed her on the cheek.

"At least the chickens didn't freeze last night. Got a dozen this morning." He smiled and rinsed his hands in the wash pan, then took a towel from the counter. "Everybody up?"

She worked a spoonful of lard into the flour.

"I called them. Ain't seen them yet."

He started across the room, then paused and turned to her.

"What day is it?"

Her hands worked the dough in the wooden bowl.

"Tuesday."

"No. I mean the number."

"Twenty-three." She sighed. "December twenty-third."

His voice rang through the house as he turned away and moved down the hall.

"Hey! Let's go! Get up." He clapped his hands. "Time to go. Lot of work to do today."

In a few minutes the three boys wandered in. Guy took a seat at the table. Wilson scooted a chair near the stove. Clyde sat in a chair across the room along the wall near the hall.

"We get that bottom cleared up today, maybe we can go huntin' in the morning."

Wilson grumbled a response.

"No squirrel crazy enough to get out in this cold."

"I saw three down there yesterday."

Edgar came from the hallway.

"You boys need to get everything fed and ready before breakfast. We can finish up with that bottomland today. Elmer Banks wants us to bring him a load of wood."

Wilson glared at Guy.

"You could help."

Guy looked away. Clyde shoved his foot in a boot and leaned over to lace it up.

"School's his job."

Wilson scowled at him.

"I didn't get to finish."

Clyde shot him a look.

"Could have if you hadn't quit."

Edgar poured a cup of coffee.

"All right. You two can complain while you work." He took a sip of coffee and glanced at Guy. "Get that homework done?"

"Yes, sir."

Edgar slipped on his coat and spoke past him to the others.

"Let's get busy. Breakfast will be ready in a few minutes."

A cold wind swept through the room as he opened the door and stepped outside.

Clyde slipped on his other boot, tied the laces, and stood. He took his coat from a peg on the wall and started toward the back door. He rubbed Guy's head as he passed the table.

"Learn something for me." He nudged Wilson as he passed the stove. "Come on. You can feed. I'll hitch the wagon."

Wilson slipped on a coat. They started out the door. The house grew quiet.

Kathleen opened the stove and took out a pan of biscuits. She put one on a plate and set it in front of Guy.

"You all right?"

"Yes, ma'am."

She slid a jar of sorghum molasses next to the plate and laid a spoon beside it.

"Sleep well?"

"Yes, ma'am."

He dipped molasses from the jar to his plate and began to eat. She took a seat across the table from him.

"Everything okay at school?"

"Yes, ma'am."

"You sure you got your homework done?"

"Yes, ma'am."

He took a bite. She mustered a smile.

"Christmas is coming."

"Yes, ma'am."

The look in his eye sent a pang of sadness deep into her soul.

"Don't you like Christmas?"

His eyes dropped to the plate. His voice was low.

"Be better if I was gettin' something."

"Maybe you will."

He didn't reply. She stood and turned to the stove.

"Well, Christmas isn't here yet." She cracked an egg in the cast iron skillet and set it on the stovetop. "You never know what might happen."

She did her best to sound hopeful, but inside she felt herself sinking beneath a dark sea of sadness.

An hour later the house was empty. She sat alone churning butter from the milk Edgar coaxed from the cow. When that was finished she sat by the fireplace in the front room darning socks and patching their extra overalls.

Near the middle of the morning, she made a pan of cornbread and put on a pot of dried beans. Everyone would be hungry when they came in for lunch. Hungry and cold. They would need something hot to eat.

While lunch cooked on the stove, she walked outside to the chicken coop behind the barn. They needed something special for Christmas dinner. The oldest rooster would do just fine. She'd penned him up about a month ago. Since then she'd been feeding him a little more than the rest. She took an ear of corn from the crib and worked the kernels free from the cob in her hand as she made her way behind the barn.

The wind cut through her clothes. Wilson was right. It was too cold for anything to be outside. She filled the cup in the rooster's pen and hurried back inside. He was getting fat. If he didn't freeze in the next two days he'd make a fine meal.

Lunch came and went. Afternoon passed quickly. Before long, the sun began to fade toward evening. Guy came home from school. The wood box had to be filled and the washbasin needed fresh water. The chickens had to be fed once more and the cow needed to be tied in her stall. In between, she saw Guy shooting that sponge ball at the hoop above the barn door. But she didn't have time to watch for long. Edgar and the boys would be in from the field soon. They'd be tired and cold—and hungry. She took a piece of salt-cured pork from the box near the stove and rinsed away the brine. She cut it into pieces, placed it in a cast iron skillet, and smothered it in onions. While it simmered on the stove, she took down the bowl from the cabinet and began kneading the dough for a batch of biscuits.

After supper Guy brought his books from the bedroom and sat by the kerosene lamp at the kitchen table. He opened a math book and began doing homework. Clyde wandered into the front room and lay on the floor near the fireplace. Wilson put on his coat and walked out the front door.

When the table was cleared Edgar took his coat from a peg by the door.

"I'm going out to the barn."

He opened the door and stepped outside.

A few minutes later, Kathleen wrapped herself in a blanket and followed him outside. She found him working in the dim light of a lantern at an anvil near the back of the barn. Lumps of coal glowed red hot in a small forge that stood nearby. He held a narrow strip of steel in the grip of long-handled tongs and pounded it on the anvil. The ringing sound made her jump with each swing of the hammer. He glanced up as she approached. She gave him a smile.

"What are you doing?"

"Fixing this hoop."

"What for?"

"It needs fixing."

She nodded. He pounded on it a few more times, then shoved it beneath the coals in the forge and worked the crank on the billows. The coals glowed bright. The steel turned orange, then red. He drew it from the forge and laid it on the anvil.

"I figure I'll get 'bout two dollars for that load of wood tomorrow."

She did her best to sound pleased.

"Good."

He pounded the metal, looked at it once more, then pounded it again.

"We need anything. Flour? Sugar?"

"Shoes."

He struck the metal.

"Shoes?"

"The boys need new shoes."

Edgar pounded the metal again, then shoved it back in the red-hot coals of the forge. Kathleen drew the blanket tighter around her shoulders.

"And tomorrow's Christmas Eve."

Edgar cranked the billows.

"Clyde needs some shotgun shells."

She frowned.

"For Christmas?"

"Puts food on the table."

"Doesn't seem like much of a gift."

"What'd you have in mind?"

"I don't know. Maybe a nice shirt."

He gave her a quizzical look.

"You make his shirts."

"I make shirts from sack cloth."

He drew the strip of metal from the forge and laid it across the rounded end of the anvil, then gently tapped it into a circle.

"Not much difference if you're working in the field."

"I think he'd like one for Emma."

"Emma?" He glanced up at her between swings of the hammer. "Emma who?"

"Emma Norton." Kathleen smiled. "You should see the way he looks at her."

The strip was now a hoop about two feet in diameter. He moved it from the anvil to the forge and once again shoved it into the coals.

"I've seen it."

She nodded to the forge.

"That a barrel hoop?"

"No."

He cranked the billows. She leaned against a post.

"Wilson wants a hat."

"What kind of hat?"

"A man's hat."

Edgar drew the hoop from the forge with the tongs. He squeezed the ends together until they overlapped, then held them against the anvil and pounded the ends together with the hammer.

"What do you want?"

"I want a ball for Guy."

Edgar smiled.

"A ball?"

"Like they use for basketball."

Edgar chuckled.

"You've never seen a basketball game."

"Yes, I did. Once. When I was a girl."

"Where?"

"Carrollton. They were playing behind the school."

Edgar looked the hoop over, then dropped it in a bucket of water. Steam rose in the air. He smiled at her.

"That's a lot of dreams for two dollars."

Kathleen sighed. Edgar glanced at her.

"How's that rooster?"

"He'll be ready. If he doesn't freeze."

"Not that cold."

"Seems like it's as cold as the North Pole."

Edgar banked the coals against the back of the forge and took the lantern from its hook on a rafter above his head.

"Come on. We better get inside. Time for those boys to be in bed."

❧

The next day was Christmas Eve. There was no school. After breakfast, Clyde and Guy hitched the mule to the wagon and loaded it with firewood, then helped Wilson feed the animals. When they were finished, Clyde came inside for the shotgun. Kathleen sat by the fireplace in the front room sewing a square for a quilt top.

"Where you going with that?"

"Get us a squirrel for supper."

"Be back by noon."

"Yes, ma'am."

The back door banged closed. The house was quiet.

After a while, she laid the sewing aside and walked to the kitchen. She took a few sticks of wood from the box by the door and stoked the fire in the stove. A pan of cornbread. Another pot of dried beans. She gave herself a cup of coffee and added a spoon of sugar. It was Christmas Eve.

In a little while, the boys returned. Guy ran in, excited.

"Clyde shot three squirrels."

"Good. He can clean them too."

"Can you make a stew?"

"I suppose."

"Where's Daddy?"

"Took that load of wood to Elmer. Haven't seen him all morning."

Guy frowned at her.

"He ain't back, yet?"

"No."

"He could have taken three loads by now."

"Probably just visiting."

When they finished eating, the boys hurried outside. Kathleen cleared the table and washed the dishes, then returned to the front room and the sewing. She glanced out the window and let her eye search down the red dirt road. Guy was right. Edgar should have been back a long time ago.

In a little while Clyde brought her the squirrels. She cut them in small pieces and browned them in a skillet, then dropped them in the stew pot. A few potatoes. A wrinkled carrot. And they called it a stew. She moved the pot to the back of the stove and let it simmer.

Through the back window she saw Guy with the foam ball shooting it toward the makeshift hoop above the barn door. She stirred the stew and returned to the sewing in the front room.

The sun was beginning to set when the front door opened. Edgar glanced at her as he stepped inside, surprised to see her there.

"Hey."

Her eyes never looked up.

"You missed lunch."

He moved across the room. Under one arm he held a cardboard box. In the other, a large sack stuffed full. He grinned at her as he disappeared down the hall. She heard the rustle of the bag and the sound of the box as he slid them under the bed. An amused smile spread across her face.

She stood and walked to the kitchen. In a moment, he appeared behind her at the stove. She resisted the urge to ask about the sack and box.

"You have a good visit with Elmer?"

"Huh?"

"You been gone a long time for one load of wood."

He smiled at her.

"Yeah. We had a good long visit."

"Drink a lot of coffee?"

"Not much. Anything left from lunch?"

She gave him a look.

"You mean you sat over there all this time and they didn't feed you?"

He opened the pie safe and took out a piece of cornbread. After a bite or two he opened the door and stepped outside.

Just after dark, Clyde and Wilson came in the front door carrying a large cedar tree with a wooden support nailed to the end. They squeezed it through the door and set it in front of the window next to the chair where Kathleen had been sewing. The tree was tall and round. The tip of it touched the ceiling. Kathleen came from the kitchen and stood at the doorway by the hall.

"That's a nice one. Where'd you find it?"

Clyde grinned.

"By that bottom we've been clearing. Next to the river. We found it the first day. Daddy said you'd like it."

A smile spread across her face.

"He did, did he?"

"Yes, ma'am."

She turned away and moved across the kitchen to the stove. She lifted the lid on the stew pot and stirred it with a large metal spoon. Just then, the back door opened. Edgar and Guy appeared.

"Brrr. Be another cold night tonight." Edgar rubbed his hands together and moved close to the stove. "That stew smells good."

He reached to lift the lid on the pot. Kathleen slapped his hand away. He frowned at her. She gave him a smile and handed him a stack of plates.

"Put these around the table."

Edgar took the plates.

After supper Kathleen found a jar of popping corn and popped it in a pan on the stove. When it was ready, she strung it on a thread with a sewing needle. Clyde and Guy hung the strands around the tree. While they did that, she brought a box of decorations from the bedroom. Edgar glanced at her.

"I hope you didn't peek."

From the corner of her eye she saw the look on Guy's face. She smiled at Edgar.

"I never peek."

She handed Guy a red glass ball.

"Hang this one near the middle. And be careful. It was my mother's."

She turned to Wilson and gave him a green one.

"Put this one on the side near the window."

One by one she handed out the balls. Each one placed in a special spot on the tree. Before long the cedar was dotted with red, blue, and green balls that hung between strands of popcorn garland. At the top was a cardboard star wrapped in tin foil. When they were finished, Edgar and Kathleen sat in the chairs and sipped coffee. The three boys stretched out on the floor and stared up at the tree.

It was late when the last log on the fire in the fireplace crumbled to a pile of coals. As the coals sank beneath the ashes, Edgar stood.

"Time for bed."

Outside, the wind picked up. A chill settled through the room. Kathleen scooted the boys down the hall. She lingered a moment with them. A word with Clyde and Wilson. Tucking the quilts in tight around Guy.

Satisfied it had been a good evening for them, she made her way down the hall and sat on the edge of the bed. She brushed her hair in the dark until her fingers were cold and stiff. Finally, she crawled in bed beside Edgar.

When he left the house that morning she knew he was going much farther than Elmer Banks' house. She'd lived with him a long time. There wasn't much about him she didn't know. The box beneath the bed held a hat for Wilson. Somewhere in that sack was a shirt for Clyde and a ball for Guy, and who knows what else. Maybe even a pair of shoes. She hadn't peeked. She just knew it. But she'd wondered all evening how he did it. How he'd taken two dollars and turned it into all that.

The wind outside howled around the corner of the house. A chilling draft seeped through the cracks between the boards in the wall. She pulled the covers up around her ears and lay there thinking.

Outside, the bright winter moon rose in the night sky sending moonlight streaming through the window. In the gray glow, details of the room emerged from the darkness. Her eyes wandered from the foot of the bed to the dresser along the wall. The mirror above it. The picture of her parents on the wall across from the window. Near the door was the chair with Edgar's overalls hanging on the back. Her eyes ran along the blue denim fabric and followed the orange stitching that outlined the pockets and the buttonhole near the strap on the left side. In the moonlight she could see the buttonhole, its edge worn smooth where Edgar's watch chain had once rubbed against it.

The watch chain. And the watch that had once belonged to his father.

CREDITS

"Christmas Express" by Sigmund Brouwer. © Sigmund Brouwer. All
rights reserved. Reprinted by permission.
Illustrated by Paul Segsworth.

"A Cardinal, Bloodred" by Wanda Luttrell. © Wanda Luttrell. All
rights reserved. Reprinted by permission.
Illustrated by Helen Harrison.

"Broken Pieces" by T. L. Higley. © T. L. Higley. All rights reserved.
Reprinted by permission.
Illustrated by Bob de la Peña.

"Poinsettia Parable" by Angela Elwell Hunt. © Angela Elwell Hunt. All
rights reserved. Reprinted by permission.
Illustrated by Susan Vannaman.

"Mary" by Mike Nappa. © Nappaland Communications Inc. All rights
reserved. Reprinted by permission.
Illustrated by Dale Johnson.

ABOUT THE AUTHORS

SIGMUND BROUWER is a best-selling novelist and popular Christian author of many books, including *The Weeping Chamber* (Tyndale House) and the novella *Pony Express Christmas* (Tyndale House).

WANDA LUTTRELL was born and raised in Franklin County, Kentucky, where she lives with her husband, John. Her writing has appeared in various Christian and general-market publications, and she is the author of fourteen published books, including the suspense novel *The Dandelion Killer* (Promise Press) and the award-winning novella collection *Simply Christmas* (Barbour).

T. L. HIGLEY is an author whose lifelong interest in history and mythology has propelled her into ancient worlds to shine the light of the gospel into cultures of the past. She is the author of the popular suspense novels *Retrovirus* (Promise Press), *Marduk's Tablet* (Barbour), and *Fallen from Babel* (Creation House). Visit T. L. Higley on the Web at www.TLHigley.com.

ANGELA ELWELL HUNT is a Christy award-winning novelist who writes books for everyone who wants to expect the unexpected. With more than three million copies of her books sold worldwide, she is the best-selling author of *The Tale of Three Trees* (Lion), among other titles. Visit Angela Hunt on the Web at www.angelahuntbooks.com.

MIKE NAPPA is a best-selling and award-winning author of many books, including *The Courage to be Christian* (Howard Publishing) and *Tuesdays with Matthew* (RiverOak). Visit Mike's agent on the Web at www.SteveLaube.com.

JANICE THOMPSON is a Christian author from the Houston area who spends her days writing Texas-based novels, including *Hurricane* (RiverOak). To learn more about her books, visit her Web site, www.janiceathompson.com. She loves to hear from her readers and can be reached at booksbyjanice@aol.com.

JOHN DUCKWORTH is an editor in Colorado Springs, Colorado. He is the author of several books, children's videos, and church dramas.

JOHN DESIMONE is a gifted storyteller and author of the novel *Leonardo's Chair* (RiverOak). He makes his home in California, where he is a member of the California Writer's Club of La Habra.

JACK CAVANAUGH is the author of twenty published novels, including An American Family Portrait series (RiverOak), and has received acclaim from both Christian and mainstream organizations for excellence in fiction. He and his wife, Marni, live in Southern California.

TERRY BURNS is a Vietnam veteran and the author of the Mysterious Ways series (RiverOak). He has seventeen books and over two hundred articles and short stories in print, and his writing is often characterized as "Inspirational Fiction with a Western Flair." Visit Terry on the Web at www.terryburns.net.

ROBIN JONES GUNN is a best-selling and award-winning author of more than sixty books, including the Glenbrooke series (Multnomah) and the Sisterchicks series (Multnomah Fiction). She and her husband, Ross, make their home in the Pacific Northwest. You can learn more about Robin at www.RobinGunn.com.

JOE HILLEY is the popular author of the novels *Sober Justice, Double Take,* and *Electric Beach* (all RiverOak). You can read more about him at www.joehilley.com.